Conversation
Skills

For The Ultimate Professional

By Dan E Blaze

(A 'Master Sales Manual Series of Books)

Master Sales Manual
Series of Books

Conversation Skills is the second in the Master Sales Manual Series of Books.

All titles in this series are based on proven models and principles as found in psychology, business, and marketing and as passed on through professional training courses and seminars. You will not find any advice or suggestion skewed to my own point of view, or the point of view of others… Only cold hard facts and proven concepts. The series is designed for true professional learning without the use of lengthy stories or multiple examples. If you're ready to dive right in, with information and techniques that you can start using today, then these are the books for you!

The Master Sales Manual Series of Books will take you through a broader view of sales in order to help you develop into a more complete professional. If you've ever been in a real selling situation, then you know that there is more to sales then simply telling others all about the wonderful features and benefits of your product. Sales professionals today need to win the customer over from start to finish.

The Master Sales Manual is the ONLY book that provides an in-depth review of each of the 10 critical skill-sets necessary to become a master at the art of sales. It is essentially a text-book reference guide to sales and adjacent fields of study. It is NOT your regular sales book, and is not designed to entertain you.

The Master Sales Manual: For the Serious Professional!

Contents

Preface

I was 23 when I got into sales. My first job was selling windows for a national window company. They sat me at a desk with a little black phone, handed me the phone book, and said "ok, call people and sell them windows". Then they explained "first thing is first, set up some appointments to go visit people". "Visit who?" I asked! "Who do I call? Who wants to buy our windows" The answer that echoed to me form across the room was disappointing... "There's the phone book - Start with A". Thank God it was just a local phone book.

It was years later when I got hired with a large call-center that I received my first ounce of REAL training. How to sell... What to Say... How to Say it. They taught me to use features and benefits in succession... Give them a feature, and immediately follow up with a benefit. Just repeat this over and over. At the time, these were advanced sales skills... At least to me.

I remember reading that big companies such as Xerox and IBM would send their Sales force to be professionally trained. I remember wondering why none of the companies that I worked for (to date) had sent me to any formal sales training. I also remember asking myself over and over again how I could possibly become better at my chosen career.

As I moved from one job to another, I started paying attention to things. I would find the best seller in each job and listen closely to what he's saying, and how he's saying it... To the inflection in his voice... To the words he chose... And then I would ask a lot of questions. I would often take time out to do this when I should have been working, which caused me many disputes with management. At some point… I decided it just wasn't enough.

THE PROBLEM: Unless you work for some large corporation – Fewer and fewer companies are investing in sales training for their Sales force… And those who make an attempt to train their sales staff often provide very basic sales skills

So came the time for me to train myself. I started paying for professional training classes with my own funds. I started buying every sales book I could get my hands on. I bought audio tapes and listened to them day in and day out… And after time, some of it started sinking in. My sales skills started developing and I became a much more persuasive individual.

With so much confidence in myself, I took on opportunities as an independent salesperson with a heating and ventilation company. I was introduced to the world of DIY "Do It Yourself"...

THE SECOND PROBLEM! Sales skills alone, just aren't enough. You need a heck of a lot more than mere sales skills to be a well-rounded professional.

I had to create lead-lists; book appointments; plan and perform sales presentations; persuade them to buy; negotiate the offer; close the deal; and build a referral network. It may not seem like a lot, but I found it to be overwhelming for just one person.

With my new-found sales skills, I sought to teach myself everything I could about being a successful independent salesperson. Very little assistance in the matter was provided by the company (and as I moved to other positions later, I found this to be a growing trend).

I decided to spend years researching methods and techniques of honing every skill necessary to be the Perfect Sales Pro, and I wrote it all in one book entitled "The Master Sales Manual". I wrote the book as a training guide for myself. This book – Communication Skills – is the second in a series of books designed to help the average salesperson train himself to become The Perfect Sales Pro.

Acknowledgements

No-one who achieves success does so without acknowledging the help of others.

- *Alfred North Whitehead*

It is important that I acknowledge all of the resources that I have had the opportunity to learn from... The series of books, audio and video available on the market today. The teachers that have taught me, my friends, my foes, and my family. As well as the universe called the World Wide Web.

I'd especially like to thank those people in my life who have encouraged me to continue writing, have had faith in my endeavor, and pushed me in times when my morale was low. In the famous words of the Beatles: We all need a little help from our friends.

Introduction

We often take conversation skills for granted. We fail to put forward the conscious focus and care in our words, sentences, phrases, and overall communication… Why? My guess would be this happens because we assume that a conversation is a conversation, and since we have been conversing all of our lives, we must, by now, be masters at the subtle art. Unfortunately, we are wrong!

The intrigue and complexity that occurs within every conversation, whether it is of one minute or one hour, is incredibly fascinating, once you allow yourself to begin understanding. Our unconscious mind processes over 10,000 threads every second, or so scientists believe. That's over 400 billion bits of information. We pick up on all of the subtle things that are accepted through our five senses; things you and I probably never even notice we're doing. The brain deciphers all of these subtle cues, decides what is important and what is not, and spits an idea into our consciousness allowing us to derive meaning from these events… And it does so without asking us first!

With this in mind, don't you think you ought to be a little more careful as to how you allow others to perceive you? Don't you think you should take a little more control of the bits of information that you send out? And don't you think you could learn to understand others just a little more precisely?

By telling the conscious mind what to look for, and what is important, you allow that message to transcend into the unconsciousness. The next time your unconscious picks up on these subtle things, it will communicate back to the consciousness, and voila! You will be aware of it. You can, one step at a time, become the perfect communicator… Aware of every action they make, and every action you do.

I recommend, in addition to this book, you pick up a book on non-verbal communication (body language), as well as a book on persuasion. The unity of these three subjects can have instrumental effects on your abilities to communicate perfectly.

SPECIAL NOTE:

Throughout this book, I use a book and pen, like the one to the left. This is my attempt at jumping outside of the script and speaking to you directly. Take special notes here, and enjoy!

Chapter 1

What's The Big Deal Anyway?

Understand how communication happens:
Its processes, and coding.

$\mathcal{T}$he assumption, of course, is that we are all natural communicators… And since we are naturals, we must also be experts. I mean, if I've been speaking English my whole life, I MUST be good at it… Right?

The truth is, like anything else; if you learn to do it wrong the first time and you practice it wrong till you've perfected that, then you become an expert at doing it wrong! Now, I'm not trying to say that you're speaking methods are incorrect… I wouldn't know that… But very few individuals who have not been involved in some form of communication training have excellent conversational skills. By that I mean, perfect communication skills – For the perfect professional! Ponder upon that as you read through this book.

Communication, whether in conversation or otherwise, is a delicate intervention of representation (of ideas), meaning (associated to those ideas), and intention (of the speaker). This will be reviewed several times throughout this book. In this next chapter, we review how communication happens and why that's important.

Communication?

Communication in any form is simply the sending of signals from one source that may be understood by a second source. Communication between animals (humans included) incorporates two types of signals: Signs and Symbols…

Signs are understood because they are the result of a cause, thus our understanding of the cause allows us to easily understand the sign, and thus the message it conveys.

When a person blushes, we understand that they are embarrassed because blushing is the result of embarrassment. In conversation, when a person makes the "uhhh" sound, we understand that they are lost for words because the "uhhh" sound is the result of trying to speak when our words are lost (not literally of course).

Symbols on the other hand, are developed and understood by societies. Language is understood by those who learn and use that specific language, simply because of an implicit agreement between users of the language. There is no real reason why the sound uttered when we speak the word "baby" should refer to a new-born child, other than the fact that it has been agreed upon by English speaking societies. In other languages, the notion of a "baby" is understood by different utterances.

With all this in mind, you may now realize that you cannot not communicate. Even if you choose not to say a word, you are in fact communicating something, as the receiver of your non-communication creates interpretations and in return assimilates a response.

Reciprocity of Communication

It is important to remember that conversation must occur between two or more people… Too often, people enter a conversation for the sole purpose of doing 100% of the talking… This is not conversation – it is a monologue. Conversation occurs when two people interact back and forth, thus there is a reciprocal sequence of interactions.

Context of Communication

Since conversation may occur face to face, or it may occur through some other means, such as telephone, chat sites, email, etc. Conversation may or may not occur within a shared context. Not having a shared context may skew one's understanding of the other's meaning.

Layers of Communication

In human interaction, multiple signs and symbols are generated and combined to express single ideas; we discuss many of these signs and symbols in chapter 5. Such signs and symbols may include words and phrases, minor utterances (such as uhhh, uhmm, and ahhh), tonality, intonation, gestures and body-language, eye-gestures, and other forms of movement. Most often, words alone are not sufficient to provide an appropriate understanding of the message – words are only 'one piece of the pie' so to speak. It is thus necessary, for effective communication to take place, to understand the entire message.

This book is focuses strictly on audible conversation skills, and is not designed to provide a look at non-verbal gestures. You may want to pick-up a book on body language to acquire an understanding of non-verbal communication along with this book.

When engaged in conversation, attempt to pick up on the various layers of communication that exist so that you can better understand the total message. Check also for congruency between different layers of communication – your clients may be saying one thing, but showing something else.

The Conscious Vs. The Unconscious

We communicate both through conscious and unconscious signals, which are called cues. A "cue" is any large or small action or sound beyond the simplicity of words that can be recognized by the brain as input. This can be the moving of any part of the body (referred to as a major cue) or a more subtle movement or twitch that may not consciously be recognized (called a minor cue, often also referred to as a subtle cue). Cues send a type of signal to the receiver, who then consciously or unconsciously associates some form of meaning to it.

Let's just clarify what is defined as consciousness and unconsciousness; or what is referred to as the conscious and unconscious mind. The brain processes billions of bits of information per second - There are those things which we become aware of, and there are those things that we are completely unaware of. For example, the human heart (under normal conditions) beats somewhere in the vicinity of 100 beats per minute... Completely without the need to be aware of it, or otherwise interact in any way... It is autonomously handled by the unconscious. The oncoming of a sneeze happens in much the same way, as do breathing (in general) and reflex reactions. The body does what it needs to do based on messages that are sent to it by our brains, and we do not become aware of it until it has either happened or is happening, and in some cases not until it stops happening. These autonomous and independent activities within our brains are referred to as the unconsciousness.

Compare this to conscious activity, which is any activity that allows and/or requires you to be aware of occurrences. When you lift a coffee cup, your brain actually visualizes you doing so before you even begin to move. You are prepared for the actions that you must take, and the sensations that you are about to feel. When a ball moves toward you, you recognize that it is doing so and become aware of what is about to happen, what is happening, and what should happen to avoid injury. Your mind actually plays a sort of movie, or set of moving pictures that allow you to visualize this. This awareness is referred to as the consciousness.

> A major key to developing expert communication skills is to learn to become aware of those things you would normally be unaware of – Thus having more control of the overall message that you send to the person receiving your message. By first understanding the subtle cues of conversation, we can work toward this.

Speech Act

Whether we know it or not, every time we speak we are performing speech acts. A speech act is an act that is performed by speaking. John Langshaw Austin, a philosopher of language who also served in the British Intelligence Services MI6, made popular the term "speech act" in his book "How To Do Things With Words".

Speech act theory suggests that there are three types of forces that occur in speech, either independently or in combination, they are:

Locutionary Force

This includes linguistic properties. The words / phrases are taken in a literal sense. For example, having said "I'm hungry", I have made <u>a statement</u> in the fact that I am feeling hungry.

Locutionary force includes three main subdivisions:

*1) **Phonic:*** This generally refers to the process of producing a particular sound. The phonetics of speech.

*2) **Phatic:*** The arrangement of sounds that are produced.

*3) **Rhetic:*** The structure of sentences aimed at delivering a particular message.

Illocutionary Force

This is the purpose of having said what was said. An intention is made in the performance of having spoken. Referring to our previous example, having said "I'm hungry", I could be expecting that someone give me some food, I could be suggesting that someone should tell me where I can get some food, or I may even be requesting that someone suggest to me what I should eat (especially if I am not familiar with the surrounding area).

Illocutionary force can be one of five distinguished classes:

*1) **Assertives:*** Speech acts where the speaker asserts his opinions.

*2) **Directives:*** Speech acts that seek to cause the listener to engage in some form of action (i.e. requests, commands, advice, etc.).

*3) **Commissives:*** Speech acts that commit the speaker to some future action (i.e. promises, oaths, guarantees).

4) Expressives: Speech acts that express the speaker's emotions and attitudes (i.e. Congratulations, excuses, thanks, etc.).

5) Declarations: Speech acts that seek to change the context of reality, these are usually done only by individuals who have the power to do so (i.e. baptisms, pronouncing someone guilty by law, pronouncing holy union in marriage, etc.).

Perlocutionary Force

This is the effect or result that is produced, either on the speaker himself, or on the listener. Again with the example "I'm hungry", the perlocutionary force could that of inspiring someone to see it in themselves to buy me lunch (I'd really like that!).

Conversational Stance

Conversation, through its many communicative techniques, expresses the stance of both speaker and listener. Stance is the position that a speaker takes in conversation, and may be extended to include the position taken by the listener as he generates a response to the speaker. In other words, stance is the combined influence of a person's attitudes, opinions and perspective as displayed through their communication.

Stance is displayed through a variety of symbols and signals, the most common of which being body language, tone, volume, use of words/phrases, and emotional input. There are two subcategories of stance, they are:

1) Epistemic Stance: This is essentially the manner in which the speaker displays his knowledge and certainty of the information contained within the conversation. The more knowledgeable a speaker appears, and the more certain he appears that his knowledge is correct, the stronger his epistemic stance.

2) Affective Stance: Affective stance has to do with the emotions portrayed by a speaker, and the manner in which those emotions interact with the listener(s). It is sometimes thought to be a perspective on the personality of the speaker; however, this is not always the case.

The Communication Process

Communication doesn't just happen. It isn't some chaotic event that has no flow or structure. There is a flow to which all communication takes place. Sociologists have broken down the communication process into five basic stages:

The Sender

The first part in the communication process begins with you – The sender. Two different people could have the same thought, but ultimately intend on sending distinctly different messages. This has a lot to do with personality, values, morals and beliefs.

The Message

The message is the idea that you intend to get across. What's important to recognize here is that when you decide to speak, you are verbalizing ideas that have formed in your mind? Studies have shown how people form some imagery in their mind and then attempt to describe that imagery verbally. Further studies have even shown how letters and words are recognized as images, and our brain merely decodes the ideas represented by those images (letters and words), either individually or in groups. All this being said, it is the idea that you form in your mind that changes what is said, and it all starts with you. If you can create better images and learn to better verbalize those images, then you have taken the first step to better communication.

Encoding

Encoding is the verbalization of the image or images in your head. Sometimes, the message we <u>want</u> to send is not necessarily the message we send. There are several reasons for this, beginning with our ability to convert ideas into words, our use and familiarity with the language we are using (which may not always be English), as well as the size of our vocabulary and the words and phrases we have learned to use.

Recognizing the need to ensure uniformity in sending effective messages, Scott M Cutlip and Allen H Center developed the 7 C's of effective communication in 1952. They suggested that all messages should be clear, concise, concrete, correct, coherent, complete, and courteous.

Channel

The Channel is the medium we use to communicate our message. This may be spoken word, written word, audio, telephone, video, hand-signals; etc. For our purposes we will focus only on the spoken word. The channel can also consist of imperfections, as well as noise (background distractions).

Decoding

The message we send is not always the message received. As the message is received by another individual, his brain

> The Single Biggest Problem In Communication, Is The Illusion That It Has Taken Place
> - *George Bernard Shaw*

will break down the message into individual parts. The originally intended message is now skewed by additional non-verbal content that was picked up when the message was sent by complications in the encoding phase, as well as by issues in the channel such as any imperfections and background noise. The message may also be distorted by reference to context, as the same message under two different circumstances may be perceived as two distinctly different messages.

Receiver

Just like you, the sender of the information, an individual in their own rights, may send some subtle cues in their message based on their personality, values, morals, beliefs, and so on. The sender also skews the information received and decoded according to their own personality, values, morals, and beliefs, as well as their understanding of the information received and the meaning interpreted by that information.

Feed-back

The receiver of the information then sends feedback in the form of either verbal or non-verbal cues, or both. This is an unconscious response to the information received, and may be as subtle as the twitching of an eye, or a short ummm or ahhhh. This is not the same as a reply to the original message. A reply would essentially be a message in itself. This is an unconscious feedback that often occurs without the receiver recognizing that it has occurred.

Noise

In the communication process, there will also exist noise – Internal or external sounds that act as a barrier to effective communication. There are three types of noise to be concerned with:

1) Physical Noise: Physical noise occurs in the environment (i.e. the wind, children playing down the street, the sounds of rush hour traffic, etc.).

2) Semantic Noise: Semantic noise originates from the sender of a message in the form of ambiguity and/or miscommunication (see "specificity in chapter 6). Since communication involves a combination of words and grammar (as well as other things) to produce an intended meaning, it is possible that the words and grammar used may be misleading.

For example: In Toronto, Canada I once witnessed the opening of a new Chinese restaurant that raised a huge banner in front of the store reading "Children Half Price" – It dawned on me that while I understood they meant to say "children can dine for half the price", the sign may have been read as "children are sold for half price".

3) Psychological Noise: Psychological noise begins with the receiver of a message. This results from preconceptions, biases and other mental filters that skew the original message. We'll learn more about biases and mental filters in chapter 2.

4) Self-Talk

Another form of psychological noise is what we call "Self-talk". This occurs when the receiver has a conversation within his own mind, often making judgments of the sender or the message sent by the sender, while the sender is talking. Self-talk prevents the message from being properly heard and/or understood. It often, however, occurs as a natural process and is difficult to eliminate.

Communication Orientation

The messages that we send are not always based on factual description. We speak in terms of our understanding, or abstraction of the ideas we want to portray, and these abstractions may occur in one of three ways:

Object-Oriented (In reference to objects)

This is where communication occurs regarding tangible objects. We speak about facts such as size, color or shape, quantity, etc. Here, we are not attempting to convey our emotions or how we feel, nor do we attempt to stray from the facts as we see them.

The key distraction here is the advent of perception… What I see as blue, you may call green. What I consider warm, you may consider cold. What I consider normal, you may consider abstract, abnormal or maybe even weird. This affects not only the words we choose and the way in which we structure or organize those words, but also the subtle verbal and non-verbal cues that are inevitably picked up by the unconscious mind of the receiver.

People tend to employ several types of mental

filters when talking about objects. Such filters as biases and opinions often take place here. We will review these later in this book.

Experience-Oriented (In reference to experiences)

Here, we communicate about experiences. This type of communication is primarily emotional as we attempt to describe or relate the information that has been absorbed by our five senses, and/or the emotions that we feel. We often use experience-oriented communication when we speak about events that have occurred, or are occurring, but also with events that have not yet happened, projecting the way we would feel if they did. We do this by associating those future events with our recognition of similar past events, assuming that we would feel the same way (which is not always the case).

Again, perception takes its place... Two people could be in the same situation and experience the same things, however, the outcome will differ based on each person's perception of the experience. This happens largely due to personality differences and previous experiences.

> We often tend to base current circumstances on previous experiences. Be cautious of communication in which old experiences are being applied to new situations.

Concept-Oriented (In reference to concepts or ideas)

The concept-oriented communication is where we communicate about ideas, thoughts, and concepts. Normally, this type of communication involves broad generalizations or non-specific details designed to give the receiver an understanding of the idea. This is the same as the previously stated "generalizations".

It is in reference to concepts that people are most imaginative. Sometimes, however, imagination can take precedence over reality, and we fail to view our conversation from a logical perspective.

Transition of Communication Orientation

Conversation rarely occurs in one orientation alone… We may begin a conversation with a concept-orientation and then transition to an object-orientation to provide greater detail of the concept, or possibly to the experience-orientation to either explain our own experiences or tell the listener what they could experience. In ordinary conversation, we are likely to weave in and out of each of these three communication-orientations. However, many people tend to speak predominantly in one or the other. This can give a great understanding of how information is processed, as well as what is most important to each person.

Turn-Taking

Conversation is not simply the act of communicating… I can communicate something with you, but that's not necessarily an act of conversation… One of the main ideas that make conversation different is that of turn-taking – People involved in a conversation take turns to speak. This is kind of like a conversation dance where you lead and I follow, then I lead and you follow… Or at least that's how conversation should be.

Turn-taking, however, doesn't always work the way it should in a perfect world. Some people tend to talk more than they should, and others not enough. Sometimes, a single conversation between two people occurs as two separate monologues happening simultaneously.

Axioms of Communication

Paul Watzlawick, an Austrian-American family therapist, psychologist, communications theorist, and philosopher listed five axioms of communication – Aspects of communication that exist regardless of our direct input… They just are, and there's nothing we can do about it.

1) One Cannot Not Communicate.

As long as people are aware of each other, any perceivable behavior, including the lack or absence of action or speech, may be interpreted by others as having some meaning. For example, if you happen to walk into a room, and found me in the middle of the room lying on my back, not moving, not saying anything, changes are I'm sending you a message – Call the ambulance!

2) Every communication has a content and relationship aspect such that the latter classifies the former and is therefore a meta-communication.

Everybody responds differently to what is said depending on the type and quality of the relationship. The same sentences, such as "You look very sexy today" may be perceived differently from if sent from a husband to a wife, as opposed to from a stranger.

3) The nature of a relationship is dependent on the punctuation of the partners' communication procedures.

In this statement, the "punctuation" refers to the w, ay in which messages are organized and grouped into meaning, including both verbal and non-verbal messages… This is analogous to the punctuation of written communication.

A communication event (say between two people) is viewed as a set of messages being sent and received back and forth between the parties involved… As action and reaction (one thing happens and a reaction occurs because of it). Since every person communicates differently, the relationship itself can be dependent on how each person views the way in which the overall communication is organized. For example: If a one person is upset and the other is avoidant, which is the result of which… Is the first person upset because the second is guilty, or is the second avoidant because first is upset?

4) Human communication involves both digital and analogic modalities.

The terms used here may need some translation as they are denotative terms. Much as with computer technology where digital information is precise and clear, and analogue information is sent through a noisy medium; "digital", here, means clear and precise communication such as specific strings of words or gestures with generally agreed meaning, and "analogue", here, refers to

5) Inter-human communication procedures are either symmetric or complementary, depending on whether the relationship of the partners is based on differences or parity.

Symmetric interchange of communication occurs when both parties in the communication or relationship appear to have equal levels of power, or treat each other as though they did... This does not necessarily mean that they are equal in all sense of the meaning, as two individuals with different strengths (i.e. a doctor and a scientist) can communicate on a level of equal power. Complementary interchange of communication occurs when one person appears to have a great level of power, and the other less (i.e. an employer and an employee). In each of these circumstances, the type of communication, the words and phrases, tonality, non-verbal communication, etc. will be different.

> "Effective communication is 20% what you know and 80% how you feel about what you know"
>
> - *Jim Rohn*

Chapter 2

Why Aren't You Listening To Me?

*Learn How Communication Problems
Occur, and What To Do About Them.*

$\mathcal{S}$ometimes it seems like people aren't listening to you. You pour your heart out and the response that you get just is not what you had expected. This often happens because of a miscommunication, which may or may not be your fault. There are a host of obstacles that can prevent your message from being clearly understood; some of these are listed below. Having a better understanding of the obstacles in communication can not only give you a broader insight as to why your communication attempts are or are not effective, but also provide you with some indication of ways that you can communicate more effectively. This chapter is designed to make you aware of the many complications that exist in communication, including ordinary day to day conversation.

Intent

Intention is the mother of all creation. We don't always communicate with the same intent. We often trick ourselves into believing that we have something important to say... But deep inside we communicate for other reasons. The reason for communicating with others affects the way communication takes place.

> The man who is intent on making the most of his breaks is too busy to bother about luck.
> - *B. C. Forbes*

Communicative Intent

The study of communicative intent is primarily restricted to child psychology, because as children learn to communicate properly (in any language) they tend to use actions and minor vocal sounds to exhibit their desires. A child standing by the refrigerator glaring patiently at his mother is a classic sign that the child is hungry. When they point at something, possibly making vocal sounds such as "uhhh", this means that the child wants the thing that they are pointing to.

The understanding, of course, is that as we grow older, we learn to communicate effectively and such previous habits of communication are disregarded. Unfortunately, this is not always the case, and the need to understand the intent of communication is just as important in adults as it is with children.

In adults, the intent of communication is not always understood, and rather than asking, "What is it you're trying to say?" (Or something that effect), we tend to make assumptions as to the intent of communication attempt based on our understanding or perception of the total message. This makes it extremely important to be cautious of both the messages we send and the way in which the receiver may understand the message.

A Common Intent

If I am talking to you because I have some very important information to convey, and you don't really feel like conversing with me but do so only to keep good relations, the quality of the communication dwindles – What I say is likely to have a lesser impact on you… If any at all! My reason for communicating and your reason for listening do not match.

While it is not always necessary for two people to have the same intent in communicating with each other, it sure does make a big difference.

Communicative intent is taken from two points of view: That of the speaker and that of the listener. From the point of view of the speaker, it may make sense to ensure that the listener is beginning the conversation from a common point, by pre-empting the conversation using statements that begin with "I have something very important to say" or "This is important…"

From a listener's point of view, take notice of the non-verbal communication used, the tone of voice, and other cues that may show intent. Pay special attention to body language, especially forward movement, hand gestures and micro-gestures surrounding the eyes and mouth.

Receptivity

One important concept to consider throughout each conversation is that the way you communicate with others will generally have a direct effect on their perception of you, your message, and your intent. In this regard, the way that you communicate with others will also (generally) have a direct effect on the way in which they respond. This is true in all forms of communication.

Conversational Implicature

To understand a person's communication within the context of conversation, you can't simply take the literal sense of what is said. You need to understand the intentions of the speaker. The effects of such attributes as tonality, inflection, pace, and so on, must be taken into account. Take the following example for instance

"Can you close the door?"

This question can be understood in different terms depending on the receiver's evaluation of the intentions of the speaker. For example:

1) "Can you" can be understood as "are you able to", thus the question is understood as "are you able to close the door?"

2) The speaker may also have the intentions of wanting the door closed, thus the question is not actually a question at all", rather a polite way of asking for the door to be shut.

3) The speaker's intentions may also be directed at some other event, thus the question may be an indirect statement such as "it's too loud out there" or "I need some privacy".

[See also Chapter 3 "Meaning & Purpose"]

Why We Speak

Conversation is not always initiated for the same reasons. A mismatch in communication occurs when two people hold a conversation with contrasting intent. Such conversations cannot move forward in an easy and continuous stream because each party makes attempt to lead and/or sustain the conversation in accordance with their intent. Rather than engaging in such a mismatch of communication, begin by understanding and matching the other party's intent, and (if warranted) slowly lead them in the direction you want.

For example: If you and I engage in a conversation and my intent is to convey information about my new product, while your intent is to seek information about some other topic, you are likely to slowly drift out of the conversation (and perhaps daze into space) if the information that I am conveying does not match what you are seeking to know. It would make more sense for me to begin by first asking what you are seeking to know, next provide you with relevant information, and then 'naturally' lead the conversation toward the information I wish to convey.

If you were engaging in conversation for the purpose of self-interest (talking about yourself and your own personal interests), and I wished to persuade you about something, you would be less likely to listen to my message because of your own personal agenda. But if I was to first satisfy your need for self-interest (even briefly), you would then be more likely to be attentive to my message of persuasion as a display of reciprocity would take place – I listened to you, so you'll listen to me.

Below we discuss some of the most common reasons why communication is initiated.

Conveying Information

Sometimes we communicate because we have something important to say. We may also wish to convey information simply to share our thoughts and ideas.

Information Seeking

While we often wish to share information with others, we may also communicate in order to receive information... Information about our interests, information about others, and information about the world around us. As we receive and process such information, we become more confident that we are able to deal with current or upcoming situations. We may also use this knowledge to grow as people, seeking greater levels of self-esteem and/or self-actualization.

Self-Interest

Sometimes people talk simply because they like to hear themselves talk... They like to talk about themselves, they like to talk about subjects of interest, and sometimes they don't even care how interested others are in their conversation. They may even just assume that whomever they are speaking to will be interested in the topic for one reason or another. It is often in these situations that others use a relationship-listening intent and filter out much of the conversation.

Relief From Reality

We often engage in communication with others simply as a relief from reality, or for entertainment. Such conversations as verbal games, story-telling, humor and comedy (jokes) and other types of imagination are examples of this. These forms of conversation are important as they provide a form of stress-release therapy as we momentarily escape from the world (in a manner of speaking).

New Experiences

It is human nature to constantly seek out new experiences. This need is inherent in all of us from the day that we are born. As we experience new things, our brains are allowed to grow and our minds are allowed to imagine; experiences shape both our cognitive abilities as well as our creative abilities. As experiences are repeated, they become part of our identity, allowing us to better understand ourselves, our interests and desires – And this aids to shape us as individuals.

When we engage in conversation with others, we not only have the opportunity to experience new things in the conversation itself as well as the interaction with others (sometimes good, sometimes bad), but we also learn through the shared experiences of those others. We consciously and unconsciously watch and listen for various cues that bring intellectual and emotional stimulation, and often absorb these second-party experiences as our own.

Networking

Many theories in child psychology suggests that as we grow within the womb of our mothers, we develop a bond, or human-connection, that gets carried on in our infancy and as we begin to grow. This inherent need for human-connection remains with us as we grow, so that as we begin to notice that our mothers can no longer fulfill all of our needs, we seek that fulfillment elsewhere through social relationships, friendships, and other interpersonal relationships.

Also, as noted above under "new experiences", it is by being connected with others and experiencing new things through those connections that we learn to understand ourselves.

Influence

We are all social beings, and communication is a means in which we can exercise our influence on other people. As we do so, we create relationships and rapport as others become more like us. We may also gain emotional satisfaction in knowing that our thoughts and ideas are being spread.

Emotional Need

Emotional need occurs when a lack of something exists. There are signals that get sent to the brain that tell it a lack of this "something" exists, and the brain in turn releases signals that cause a rise in emotional intensity. The more intense our emotions become, the more we feel a perceived "need". This emotional need can exist with anything… biological, social or otherwise.

We normally don't feel a need to breathe, but if we were in lack of air, we would feel the "need" for it pretty quickly and would do whatever it takes to get more of it. If you hadn't eaten today, you would soon feel hunger, and that would signal a "need" to the brain telling it you need food. This happens to me when I haven't had enough coffee! The same thing also happens with other emotions… When we feel a lack of love, for example, and the desire for love becomes more intense, we become driven to seek out a source of love. This effect is primarily an automated process that occurs unconsciously.

The desire for social connection and varying levels of interpersonal relationship can involve a host of emotional "needs", and when those needs are not met, they may become intensified and drive our actions.

Self-Esteem

The more we socialize, the more we feel "liked" by others, thus raising our level of self-esteem. Self-esteem is one of the five primary human needs as suggested by Abraham Maslow in his hierarchy of needs.

Begin every conversation by first understanding the other person's communicative intent.

Listening Intent

Now that we've covered the reasons that we engage in conversation, let's review a few reasons why we listen to others... What? You thought we all listened for the same reasons?

Before I had any professional communication training, I used to think that my friends and family listened to what I had to say for that same very <u>important</u> reason... Because they cared! If only I knew... And now that I do know, I'm always wondering if people are REALLY listening to me.

People never listen for the same reasons... And the reason for listening – the listening-intent – changes the way we listen.

Active Listening

This is what we should be doing most of the time, listening actively to what is said and the meaning behind what is said, disregarding unimportant distractions.

* As professionals, when we are listening to clients, we should always engage in active listening. Listen carefully to the words and the meaning behind those words, but also listen for major and minor cues that help to determine both the meaning behind what is said, as well as the way clients feel.

Appreciative Listening

When you watch television, listen to a song on the radio, or indulge yourself in the humor of comedy, you use appreciative listening skills. This is the act of listening for pleasure.

Comprehensive Listening

This is the act of listening due to the comprehension of what is being said. When you understand what others are saying you may become more aware of the messages being sent.

Critical Listening

Here, you listen to what others are saying in a judgmental manor. You may have preconceptions about the individual or his views on the topic which serve as biases before he even begins to speak, or you may develop these biases and judgments during the conversation. Either way, judgments and criticism are held against the speaker and/or his words.

Empathetic Listening

Other times, a listener could appear to be listening, but since the conversation is a little emotional, they are more concerned with comforting the speaker and portraying empathy than they are with really listening.

Emotional Listening

Other times, they may hear something that arouses either positive or negative emotions, and in the process of becoming emotional about that, fail to hear the remainder of the conversation.

False Listening

Sometimes people seem as if they are listening, and they may pick up a few words here or there, but truthfully they're off in some other world, have spaced

> I remind myself every morning: Nothing I say this day will teach me anything. So if I'm going to learn, I must do it by listening.
>
> *- Larry King*

out, or have submitted themselves to some deep trance. Having the appearance that they are listening, a speaker could go on forever without really knowing.

Informative Listening

Informative listening occurs when your primary concern is to understand the message or information that is being disclosed.

Partial Listening

"Partial listening", often referred to as "common listening", is what people do most of the time in their daily lives... Not really listening, but not ignoring either.

Reflective Listening

We can also listen, hearing key words that bring us back in time as we relive past memories.

Relationship Listening

Or maybe we are only mocking the listening process in order to help build a stronger relationship with the speaker.

> "Yeah I called her up, she gave me a bunch of crap about me not listenin' to her enough, or somethin'. I don't know, I wasn't really payin' attention."
> *- From the movie Dumb & Dumber*

Selective Listening

We may also listen for key content, ignoring almost everything else that is said. This may occur for several reasons. First, we may be particularly interested in certain content; the speaker may have said something during the conversation, and from that moment forward we may listen specifically for information that relates to that point of interest. We also may have initially entered the conversation with the goal to seek particular information, and so our selective perception allows us primarily to focus on, and become attuned to, information that is relevant to that goal.

Hearing Issues

As two people stand side by side and hold a private conversation, they may both believe that every word, every utterance and every sound is being drawn in by the other, and that their conversations are in fact being heard. Neither of the two may consider that hearing is not always as natural a process as we may think. For some, and often for most, there are complications that may arise…

Hearing Impairment

I grew up as a child with a slight hearing deficiency in my right ear. By the time I reached grade 3, teachers were beginning to wonder why I didn't listen so well, and of course, they were all but certain that I was just lazy (which I am) and simply ignored the majority of their lectures in front of the classroom (which I didn't). It was at this point that my parents took me to a hearing specialist who was able to decipher that I had issues hearing out of my right ear. As I returned to school, they sat me on the right side of the classroom with my left ear facing the teacher, so that I may hear better – Of course, they mistakenly forgot that I honestly was lazy.

As we take on conversation with others, we often assume that they are perfect in hearing. We assume that others in this world are similar to ourselves, and unless we have dealt with difficulties, we often do not consider that others may have them. In conversation, the hearing impairments that others trifle with can cause a breakdown in the communication process.

Message Intensity

I find a lot of women are quiet speakers, and some men too… Sometimes they are quiet speakers by nature, and sometimes they are only quiet in particular circumstances. One of the little secrets that I found through conversation is that people often speak certain words a little more quietly than others, including when they are either unsure of themselves or when they are trying to hide something. Regardless of the reason… The intensity of the message, either in whole or in part, will affect the way it is heard and the receiver's ability to hear it. It may also affect the perception that is held of the conversation (in whole or in part).

Poor Listening Habits

Some people just don't listen very well… They've had poor listening skills since their younger days, and have carefully developed those poor skills throughout the years into even worse listening skills. The good news is, with a little bit of practice and attentive behavior, those poor skills can be reformed.

Recognize that hearing issues exist. It is for this reason that effective communication skills are needed. In chapter 3 we review techniques to overcome these issues and aid in ensuring the right message is understood

.

Attending Problems

I'm a big believer in customer service. This is possibly because I've been in sales for almost 20 years (at the time of writing this book) and believe that sales and customer service go hand in hand. That's why I find it so interesting that most major retail corporations spend so little time developing the customer service skills of their employees. In specific, their ability to pay attention to the needs and desires of their customers.

My biggest pet peeve is having to repeat myself... I don't mind repeating myself if it is necessary, but I don't like to do it if I feel like you just weren't listening the first time! Too often I walk into a retail store and the person behind the counter asks "Can I help you?", and just as I begin to speak they turn around and throw all of their attention somewhere else. If you ask me to speak to you, then pay attention, damn it! Is it possible it's all my fault? Maybe I just don't speak up quickly enough, and as a result counter-people think, "Gees, I seem to have a little bit of time before this guy speaks. Maybe I should be productive with my time and go do something."

Below is a list of other possible reasons why people don't pay attention to conversations:

Distractions

Our brains naturally pay attention to distractions. We are hardwired to be especially attentive to things that are out of ordinary, odd or different. When distractions happen, it takes great listening skills to ignore the distraction and focus heavily on the conversation at hand. In my early days, when I went through telephone sales training, they would have me put on a set of earphones and play a recording of two people talking in the background with a series of very distractive noises in the foreground including sounds such as dogs barking, police and ambulance vehicles driving by, and bees buzzing loudly – they were all happening at the same time. They would then quiz me on the specifics of the conversation.

There is no doubt that distractions will happen, and it is up to us to learn to ignore that which is not important, and become attentive to those things that are.

> Overcoming distraction is a learned skill. It takes concentration and practice.

Personal Agenda

Psychologists believe that we can only listen to one voice at a time. We may hear other voices, but hearing and listening are two different things.

A common mistake amongst salespeople and other business professionals is the need to tell prospects of all the wonderful attributes of their products. In plain words, many salespeople just have a really hard time shutting up! But salespeople aren't the only ones… Many people often feel they have so much to say, that while other people are speaking to them, they are rehearsing (in their minds) what they are going to say next. They have a personal agenda, in terms of the conversation, that prevents them from actively listening to what others are saying.

> Begin first by removing instances of personal agenda in your own listening skills. As a professional, you should always be employing active listening skills [discussed in chapter 4]. The next step is to work at removing the personal

agenda of your listeners – You can do this by using preparatory suggestions that will cause the listener to be more attentive, such as: "Listen closely"; "This is very important so you'll want to pay attention"; "I know you have something to say, but forget about that for a moment and listen to what I'm saying."

Ego

Conversational ego is all about power trips. Some people feel they need to be in power, and if the conversation makes them feel, in any way, that their dominancy has been suppressed or repressed, they become angry, possibly shouting mad messages quietly in their minds, which makes it very hard for them to focus on listening to anything else.

Ego can only serve to diminish the value of conversation – Learn to put your own ego aside by receiving information in an objective view. Be cautious of using language that diminishes the ego of your listeners.

Hypnotic Trance

Trances are not at all what most people think. You don't need someone to wave some shiny pendent in front of your eyes, and you don't need to drift into a zombie-like state where you don't know what is going on... As a matter of fact, most trances are actually a state of heightened awareness, where your attention is either fixated on one thing or you are attentive to the myriad of things that are happening around you. People put themselves in states of hypnotic trance every day. If you've ever jumped into in elevator and found yourself staring intently at the light that displays what floor the elevator is passing, then you were in a trance.

Trances can be brought on by anything that focuses our attention – this can be visual, audible, or some physical sensation. Once in a while (and I'll never admit this to my clients), when certain people speak to me, I find myself drifting off into a daze. Maybe it's the soothing sound of their voices, or maybe they speak in a rhythmic fashion, or maybe it's just me… But I slowly feel as if my mind is going numb, and I just want to experience that state of limbo for a while… Until something shakes me back to reality (usually it's my client saying "Are you listening to me?"). I'm sure you've felt the same way as some point in time.

Fatigue

Finally, we have fatigue. When people are tired or exhausted, their attentive abilities are lost as they attempt to reserve energy for more basic functions.

Understanding

Often enough you will find that people are listening, and may be listening attentively, but there is a lack of complete understanding which in turn makes it appear as if they were not listening in the first place. One of the issues here is that we all assume that we are great communicators (after all, we've been talking our entire lives!), and we make the assumption that we are explaining our point in a manner that is easily understood. However, just because you understand what you're talking about doesn't necessarily mean that everybody else does.

Non-Understanding

Non-understanding is when the listener does not understand what the speaker is trying to say and where no representation of the speaker's intention is formulated in the mind of the listener. Remember that we process communication in terms of abstract ideas and imagery – When the listener is not able to mentally picture what the speaker is trying to say, we have non-understanding.

With absolutely no idea of what the other person is talking about, some folks will continue on with the conversation as if all were well. They often do this because of the fear of appearing unintelligent, as it would seem if they either asked the speaker to repeat his words and/or explain himself.

Misunderstanding

Misunderstanding is different from non-understanding. It means that the listener has obtained a representation that is not in line with the speaker's intention. Essentially, he has understood something about the message that was not intended to be relayed.

Disagreement

Much of communication occurs subjectively, meaning that it is viewed or considered on a personal basis. When disagreement occurs, speakers tend to take it personally to varying degrees. Often, a small disagreement can cause a big issue in terms of understanding the remainder of the conversation

Emotional Instability

Emotional instability may be caused for a variety of reasons, including some of the reasons previously mentioned. When our emotions rise, our ability to process information on a logical platform decreases. As this happens, we may become more focused on our own emotions rather than being focused on the speaker. The more we become focused on ourselves (and our own emotions), the more our attentive abilities decline.

Inability to Empathize

People are, by nature, emotional creatures. When things go wrong, and they often do, people naturally want others to understand their situation... Not necessarily to feel what they feel, but simply to understand the way they feel. When you are unable to empathize with others, you are unable to understand the emotional state they are in. This is important as the better we can understand others, the better we can communicate on their level.

Mental State

The mental state of the listener at the time of listening may also change their ability to listen effectively. The listener may have other things that take precedence over the need to listen to the speaker, or there may be other things on in their mind.

Memory Errors

Memory errors can effect communication in both directions. They can cause loss of words or inability to clearly communicate a given point, and it can cause loss of understanding when different points or ideas need to be linked together for full comprehension of the message (if I can't remember point A, how can I link it to point B?).

Blocking

Blocking, also referred as "having a memory block" (sometimes referred to as "losing your mind"), happens when we have previously learned something, but at the time of attempting to retrieve the information we are unable to do so. We may retrieve the information at a later point, usually when we do not need to. Blocking is often caused by a second memory that is, at the time, predominantly held, causing the inability to access the first memory (the one we want).

Transience

Transience is what happens when we do not access certain information for a lengthy period of time, and we simply begin to forget. Truthfully, the brain retains the information, but the doors leading to that information (so to speak) are closed and locked. This memory may be accessed at a later point if particular triggers cause some associations that allow us to remember the "lost" information.

This type of memory loss also occurs through old age, or through various mental instabilities such as amnesia or by transient ischemic attack *(TIA - A stroke-like episode caused by problems in blood flow)*.

Absent Mindedness

Absent mindedness is when we do not pay enough attention to what is required and appear to be forgetful. We may have other things preoccupying our minds at a specific time, and ignore other things that require attention. In conversation, we may simply forget something that was recently said.

False Memories

Sometimes, we will remember something about an event that didn't actually occur. This is more common with minor facts rather than major facts. It is even possible to confuse two separate events, and mentally transfer minor facts from one event to the other. This replacement of minor details in our memory is referred to as "false memory".

Bias Imposition

People often hold different views of things… Our biases and other mental filters can skew our perception of reality so that the details of events are no longer recalled factually, but rather in a way that is congruent with the biases we hold. More on this in chapter 3.

> Learn to recognize different biases that your clients or consumers may hold, and review given information objectively.

Schematic Errors

Schematic errors are errors in memory that occur because of the schemas that we hold true. Jean Piaget, a Swiss psychologist, proposed that schematic memory errors occur in one of two ways:

1) Assimilation: This is where we seek to classify new information based on previously learned information.

2) Accommodation: Here, we acknowledge distinct differences between two pieces of information, allowing us to associate a different meaning to it.

It is thus proposed that we have a base set of understanding, and learn new information based on old information. As children, we learned that horses are animals. Children often look at a picture of a Zebra and think it's a horse, until they learn to recognize the differences and put it into a new mental category. But what if we put things in the wrong mental category? What if a child saw a picture of a giraffe and thought of it as another kind of horse? What if a customer saw a new product and classified it along with some other similar kind of products?

Misinformation

We are always accepting new information. Sometimes, new information is accepted in relation to previous memories – And sometimes, that new information changes or alters our recollection of those memories. This is common in sales and persuasion through "leading questions" or "hypnotic suggestions".

Source Confusion

This is also called "unconscious transference". People often hold memories, but fail to remember where those memories come from. For example, we may not be able to remember whether we experienced the event in person, watched it in the media, saw it in advertising, or possibly heard it through the tales of a friend. We just remember the occurrences… If the information was vivid enough we may have even created some mental imagery so strong that we remember it too.

Imagination Inflation

This occurs when our memories of an event or object appear greater than they actually were, either positively (better) or negatively (worse).

Faulty Interpretation

Faulty Interpretation occurs when we interpret what is being said incorrectly, so that our interpretation does not match the speaker's intent. This is largely dependent on both the speaker's ability to convey his message properly and the listener's ability to listen actively. There are, however, several automatic processes that cause us to skew information in one direction or the other, including the following.

Biases

A bias is a predisposed prejudice against one thing or for another. Many biases occur unconsciously, meaning that they occur without our awareness of them, and can be revealed through our communication and our actions. Studies have shown that even when people have the intention of overcoming biases, they continue to happen regardless of those intentions. More on biases in chapter 3.

Previous Experience

We build interpretation and associate meaning to all things based on our experiences and understanding of things (also see "schematic errors"). Essentially, we build mental images or maps of the different aspects of our world called "constructs", and allow those constructs to be reshaped as new information and/or new experiences become relevant.

This allows us not only to understand the world around us according to our perception of it, but also to make assumptions about future events.

This causes two main problems. The first problem exists in our inference (assumptions) about future events. Rather than re-evaluating the information that we are presented with, we base our assumptions of future events on our past experiences. By doing this, we may "skip" current information as it is omitted by the brain's mental filters. Second, as new information and experiences re-shape our constructs, the old representation of those constructs can become lost. So, the interpretation that a person may have had a year ago is no longer the interpretation they have today... And there is nothing to say that the new information that we accept is correct, or correct under all circumstances. This also leaves room for other types of abstractions like memory errors.

Congruency (Message Alignment)

When separate parts of a message or communication appear incongruent or do not match each other, we are more likely to notice. When a listener notices such a lack of message alignment, they are more likely to scrutinize the message as a whole.

Lack of congruency can occur not only in the words and sentences we speak, but within all parts of the message we send. Earlier, we discussed how in every message we send there are different cues that allow a listener to better understand the message... Such cues as voice tonality and body language must also be congruent, or in alignment, with the original message.

The best way to ensure congruency in your message is to create messages that follow a logical pattern of transitions, and ensure that your body-language and other non-verbal cues match what you're saying.

Message Collectivity

People make interpretations based on the information they have. If the listener was not able to re-collect (remember) all the information provided in a given message, they will continue to make an interpretation based on that which was remembered. The resulting interpretation, then, may be incorrect.

If you want people to make the correct assumption within a conversation, use tactics such as those covered in chapter 3 that aid in memory recall of important points.

Improper Evaluation

We all process information in our own unique way. Beyond previously mentioned mental filters, we each process information differently. Our ability to process and organize information affects our ability to learn, understand and store information.

Cognitive Ability

As we speak with others, we tend to hold an additional bias in which we believe, or want to believe, that everybody has the same cognitive abilities – The same level of intelligence, the same awareness, the same perceptions, the same...

Well, you get the point!

What "makes sense" to you, may not to others. Use phrases or questions that are designed to confirm that what you are saying is understood by the listener. This may include, "Does that make sense?" or "Is there anything that I may not have explained clearly?" NOTE: Stay away from direct statements or leading questions.

Lloyd: What do you think the chances are of a guy like you and a girl like me... ending up together?

Mary: Well, Lloyd, that's difficult to say. I mean, we don't really...

Lloyd: Hit me with it! Just give it to me straight! I came a long way just to see you, Mary. The least you can do is level with me. What are my chances?

Mary: Not good.

Lloyd: You mean, not good like one out of a hundred?

Mary: I'd say more like one out of a million.

[pause]

Lloyd: So you're telling me there's a chance... YEAH!

- From the movie Dumb & Dumber

Thought Organization

As we listen to others speak and recognize messages, cues, words and ideas, we organize these in a way that allows us to form mental imagery or ideas that in turn allow us to interpret the sender's message. From this we can associate meaning or understanding.

Most people often speak without preconception of their message or how it will be perceived by the listener. This often occurs because of speaking too quickly or simply not considering how the listener may perceive the message. Take a moment to organize your phrases. If necessary, slow down and leave pauses between sentences (strategic pauses give you time to organize subsequent phrases).

Concentrative Ability

A person's ability to concentrate and (as importantly) to focus on the message at hand influences every aspect of the communication, including our ability to organize thoughts, retain information and comprehend the final message.

Work on improving your ability to focus and concentrate on a speaker… Even in noisy situations.

Expectations

While occurrences such as attending problems, lack of understanding, memory errors, faulty interpretations and improper evaluations take place – The Receiver of a message will also develop a set of expectations regarding both the message and the speaker. These expectations usually take place as a means of measuring future occurrences - When future occurrences do not match our expectations, we become more aware and cautious.

Coordinated Management of Meaning

All individuals interact based on rules that are generally accepted by their groups or communities, which are established to help us make sense of actions and interactions within or outside of the constraints of these rules. Essentially, these rules give us a sense of what is right and wrong, what is expected and unexpected, what is right and wrong, and so on. Furthermore, these rules allow us to understand how same or similar phrases alter their meaning under differing context or circumstances.

There are six factors that alter the meaning and coherence of a message, they include:

1) Content: The content is the information that has been spoken (the words and phrases), before any sense of context is applied to it.

2) Speech Act: A speech act is any labeled action that is performed by speaking, to be understood by the receiver. This includes thanks, praise, compliments, insults, assertions, questions, etc. There are essentially two types of speech acts:

a) Illocutionary: Any speech act that is intended to make contact with a receiver.

b) Perlocutionary: Any speech act that is intended to change or alter the behavior of a receiver.

3) Episode: The episode is the situation or context in which the conversation takes place. The conversation occurs at some place, at some time, and in the context of whatever else is occurring at that particular place and time.

4) Relationship: The relationship that the two communicators have with each other. This could be, for example, a parent/child relationship, employer/employee relationship, a friendship (which could occur on varying levels of closeness), a co-worker relationship, etc.

5) Self-Concept: An individual's concept of who they are, both as an individual, as part of their group or society, and in life.

6) Culture: Different cultures have different expectations, different understandings, and different rules for social conduct and interaction. It is thus important to understand the culture or culture-mix of the conversation. In North America we are extremely multi-national, we have a very diverse mix of cultures, from state to state, or province to province – Furthermore, different regions may incorporate their own cultures.

When two people engage in conversation, each person makes an interpretation of the message and attempts to associate meaning to what the other says – The meaning we attach to the interaction is largely based on these rules of conduct. There are two different types of rules that we apply to any communicative situation.

1) Constitutive Rules: These are rules of meaning that are used to interpret or understand a message or an event.

2) Regulative Rules: Rules of action that are used to determine how to respond or behave.

Expectancy Violations Theory

Expectations are made regarding the rules of conduct, the communication, the meaning of words or phrases, and an understanding of what is appropriate or not under particular context. Those expectations are ordinarily understood in accordance with norms that may derive from society, locally, or from other groups in which the conversation takes place – and are generally contextual, meaning that they may change under different circumstances. When a speaker violates a person's expectations, it is perceived as being either good or bad (to varying degrees) depending on the receiver's perception of that speaker. When such violations are considered bad, they may lead to irritation, aggression or even anger.

A dramatic look at this may be to consider the same circumstance with two extreme variances of closeness in terms of personal relationship. If a woman was walking down the street in the middle of day and stranger walked up to her and made some derogatory remark such as "nice legs", she may take offence to such a remark. The same woman in the same situation, however, would be much less likely to take offence to such a remark if the man in question was her husband.

> It is important to understand that all communication is subject to personal evaluation.

Social incompetence

Often used interchangeably with the term social ineptitude, social incompetence refers to a lack of social skills. There are many reasons why a person may lack appropriate social skills, including a list of medical reasons. Such reasons for social incompetence may include: Autism, Attention Deficit Hyperactive Disorders (ADHD), cognitive disorders, social phobias, prior conditioning (either from family, peers, or other sources), and cultural differences.

Chapter 3

Look Into My Eyes

*Comprehend The Barriers of Attention:
How To Overcome These Barriers, & Keep
Your Listener Captivated.*

*H*ave you ever had a moment when you were in deep conversation with someone, possibly your lover, where it seemed you were the only two people in the world…? Where nothing else mattered except the words that you shared? Maybe you were captivated by each other just long enough to share a memorable moment. Maybe it was 20 minutes; maybe it was only 20 seconds… Maybe it was 2.

You can take people out of the real world and bring them into another. All you have to do is grab their attention, pull them in, and captivate them.

Captivating The Listener

In presentation psychology, there is a formula that is often used to outline the four requirements that ensure effective presentations. That formula is AIDA: Attention, Interest, Desire, and Action. The same formula can be used to understand an effective conversation. At first, it is necessary to capture the listener's attention. Once we have the listener's attention, we can then provide information that captivates the listener's interest – Without interest in the conversation, the listener will certainly not be listening for long; if they are actively listening at all. The best conversations will give the listener a desire to know more and a desire to engage in the conversation. Finally, we want the listener to respond, verbally or non-verbally, to the messages we send.

> The AIDA formula is one of the most useful formulas in sales and marketing. It can be applied to communication, presentations, advertising, sales letters, and so much more.

Getting Their Attention

OK, so you weren't listening! Maybe it's not your fault… Maybe there were things in the environment that caught your attention. Maybe your brain is hardwired to be naturally selective about what you pay attention to and what you don't, whether you know it or not. Maybe we can blame the years that passed by, or maybe we can blame the media, the news, and the rest of the world.

Actually, we can do it all. What we do or don't pay attention to is a unique combination of various factors. Each individual develops a series of mental filters that are affected by many things, including personal interest, personality, previous experiences, and the effect of second and third party input (family, friends, media, etc.). Here, we review a few of those mental filters that are most relevant to conversation skills.

Understanding Attention

In order to understand how we can gain the attention of our listeners, we must first have a basic grasp of how the brain focuses attention. Research has provided us with two main ways in which the brain decides what we focus our attention on:

1) Bottoms-Up Processing: Also called *Exogenous Processing*, this is where we selectively pay attention to something autonomously, meaning whether or not we want to. Most of the time, these are things that appear out of the norm.

2) Top-Down Processing: Also called *Endogenous Processing*, this is where we actively choose what is important to us and decide to focus our attention on it. We'll learn how we do this throughout this chapter.

Three Levels of Attention

We process information through one of three levels of attention – Externalism, where

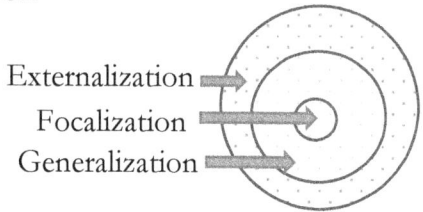

Externalization
Focalization
Generalization

we pay attention to many occurrences simultaneously (such as to our external environments); Generalization, which is what we do most of the time, not truly paying attention; and Focalization, where we focus heavily on specifics details. We may weave in and out of these three levels of attention at any given time, but we are not able to process any two levels of attention simultaneously. People feel most comfortable in a state of generalized attention, and usually can only remain in a state of Externalized or focalized attention for limited periods of time.

Techniques such as Active Listening can only be achieved through focalized attention. You need to listen carefully to the words that are spoken and audible cues that are generated as the person speaks. However, understanding the totality of the message often requires externalization, paying attention to all of the subtle non-verbal cues and gestures used by a person. In order to do both, we need to weave in and out of these two levels of attention – First focalization to externalization, and then back again.

Sohlberg and Mateer's Model of Attention

One of the most used models in clinical psychology, originally intended for evaluating patients with neurological difficulties, is Sohlberg and Mateer's model of attention. This model describes five forms of attention in growing difficulty (from 1-5), they are:

1) Focused Attention: This is the ability to focus in and pay attention to any given thing.

2) Sustained Attention: This is our ability to remain attentive or sustain the same attentional behavior during the continuous and repetitive activity of any given thing.

3) Selective Attention: Selective attention (also called selective perception) occurs when we choose, either consciously or unconsciously, to disregard certain parts of a conversation (or certain conversations as a whole). This often happens when the conversation goes in a direction that makes people feel uncomfortable; but can also happen when something in the conversation grabs our attention and/or provokes an emotional response.

4) Alternating Attention: This is the ability to shift your focus from one thing to another. It is the type of attention-processing required for multi-tasking.

5) Divided Attention: This is the most powerful type of attention-processing. It is the ability to simultaneously pay attention to two or more things equally.

Attention Span

The average attention span of an individual in regular conversion is between 5-10 seconds. That means within 5-10 seconds you had better make your point understood, before your listeners begin thinking "what the heck is it you're really trying to say?"

Attentional Bias

Attentional bias is an attention-activating filter in which we tend to be more attentive to certain information, while simultaneously being less attentive to other information. As we pay more attention to certain information we automatically place a higher value on that information, allow it to consume more of our time (especially in decision making), and consider it as being more important. Conversely, other information is deemed less important, is given a lesser value, and consumes less of our time, assuming that it is not ignored all-together.

So what information is considered important? What information do we pay attention to? Well… That is dependent of a variety of factors. If you were looking for the simple answer, you won't find it here. One of the contributing factors to Attentional Bias is personal interest: When we encounter something that we want to know more about or that affects our lives personally.

Some studies have shown that emotional states can influence Attentional Bias. When we're anxious, for instance, we are more likely to exhibit Attentional Bias early as we process information; when depressed, it may take a longer period of exposure to something before we show signs of Attentional Bias.

You can reduce the effects of attentional bias by beginning the conversation with appeal to the listener's personal interest. Causing the listener to reduce his emotional state may also aid in the matter. Use phrases such as "I have something important to review with you" or "Let's focus on this seriously for a moment."

Base Rate Fallacy

Base rate fallacy is another common bias that skews our attention to information. When presented with both generic information and specific information, people tend to favor the specific information and ignore the generic information. This means even if the generic information could potentially lead to greater benefit, and/or the specific information could lead to greater loss, we still tend to have greater faith in that which appears more certain.

A perfect example of marketing that took advantage of base rate fallacy was the advertising created for Ivory soap in the late 1800's where the soap was labeled as 99 and 44/100 percent pure. The ad did not suggest the soap was 100% pure, but left a more specific impression.

Providing specific information also affects whether or not people believe in your message. This is especially true when it comes to numbers. If I tell a client the cost of a product is $100, they are likely to think it is more than this amount and may they may even think you are omitting information (perhaps taxes or undisclosed service charges); but if I say the cost is exactly $99.24, they are more likely to believe the message. Of course, clients are likely to believe if you're willing to omit information about one thing, you must be willing to omit information about other things as well.

If you want your customers to pay attention and believe you, provide them with specific information. The more specific your message is in its entirety, the more effective it is. This is especially true with numbers, technical details, or information that is not well known.

Confirmation Bias

We make conclusions about a particular topic, and then become attracted to information confirming those conclusions. We have a tendency to also ignore or downplay any information that contradicts or does confirm the conclusions that we have established. This is closely tied to the Observer-Expectancy Effect.

Create the conclusion first. You can use effective questioning, stories and confirmation statements to help people establish the assumptions and conclusions that you want them to have. Once they hold a particular conclusion, they are likely to develop a confirmation bias to information that confirms those conclusions.

Inattentional Blindness

When we pay attention to one thing, we may miss other objects of attention that would appear obvious to others. [See "*Three Levels of Attention*" earlier in this chapter.]. Thus it must be mentioned that spending too much effort to recognize one thing, can cause a loss of perception to other things that may be just as (if not more) important.

What Are We Paying Attention To?

Attention is not black and white… What we pay attention to, and what we don't, is largely determined by our view of things… Our perception. We deem something important because it appears important to us, however, the same object may not be of any importance to the rest of the world.

Contrast Effect

People naturally think in terms of comparisons. We have been taught to do so from our early days of childhood. I'm sure you remember learning the difference between black and white, apples and oranges, or perhaps the square and round pegs (When I was a child, we had a board game to teach us how square pegs can only fit in the square holes). Through comparisons, we can understand one thing by understanding another.

When presented with two contrasting objects, our perception of the second object changes when we can immediately create a comparison to something else. If the two objects were not presented in succession, we may in fact never create a connection or develop the same degree of comparison. An illusion is thus created through the immediate comparison.

> When presenting an idea, you can alter a person's subjective perception of that idea (either good or bad) by first presenting another idea. You can either make direct comparisons, or simply leave it up to the listener to create their own comparisons. For example: If you want your offer to appear better, first present something of lesser value (either something of your own, or something by a competitor).

Conservatism Bias

Conservatism bias is about the conservation of beliefs. People tend to become fixated on their beliefs, especially if those beliefs have served them well in the past; and they generally want to continue believing that previous beliefs can be applied to new situations, which is not always the case. When it comes to changing beliefs, or to adapting our beliefs to new and different situations, most people can become resistant, even to the point of denial regarding the need to do so, before and after change becomes necessary.

If you're looking to create change, start by understanding what beliefs and values the other person holds as true, and begin your conversation from there. It is easiest to persuade others by starting where they are and working from that point. Ask questions such as "What do you think about..." or "What is your opinion of..."

Curse of Knowledge

When people have a great deal of knowledge on some topic, they hold a bias that their point of view must be correct because they have this knowledge, and can find it hard to be open-minded when others who have a lesser degree of knowledge provide their input. This bias causes a low attention span in the other person's views, opinions or input.

When you encounter a person who appears to "know it all" about the topic of conversation, giving direct information may cause confrontation as it may belittle their ego. Instead, rephrase your statements into a question, seeking their agreement.

Self-Serving Bias

People are driven toward pleasure and away from pain... We do things that make us feel good, which is primarily an unconscious behavior to avoid pain and dissonance, and this behavior causes us to view ourselves and our actions in such a way that makes us feel good… To serve our own ego or sense of self.

In essence, we create self-illusions that make us feel better about things; and may, in the process, reject input that does not make us feel good. We may reject negative feedback; or view our errors as situational or out of our control (called locus of control). We may also consider our own accomplishments as skill; even though we view the same accomplishments by others as luck (called actor-observer asymmetry).

In-Group Bias

People tend to give preferential treatment to others whom they believe are more closely similar to themselves, or part of their social groups or circles. This preferential treatment may also come across in communication, as people tend to be more accommodating, more open-minded, and generally listen better to those whom they like.

> If you're looking for preferential treatment, or if you're seeking to build strong relationships or to persuade others, begin by showing the similarities you have common and place yourself (in their mind) as being the same as they are. Focus heavily on those similarities and commonalities.

Mere Exposure Effect

Often referred to as the "Familiarity Principle", this is the effect of liking due to repeated exposure or familiarity with something. The more people are introduced to something, the more familiar it becomes to them and the more they like it.

In the 1960s, a series of laboratory experiments by Robert Zajonc demonstrated that simply exposing subjects to a familiar stimulus led them to rate it more positively than other similar stimuli which had not been presented. Miller (1976) also showed people posters about stopping foreign aid up to 200 times. They were persuaded most by moderate exposure – after 200 exposures they reacted positively to the message!

Now… Think about what advertising and TV are doing to <u>your</u> brain!

In certain cases, however, extended exposure results in annoyance and development of irritation with that exposure. This is especially true when we are exposed to things too often and too soon. Like everything, people need a little bit of time to breathe. [Also see "the familiarity principle].

Create catchphrases and bring them up often. The more those catchphrases are heard, the better they will be liked. But what's more is that your client will create an instant association between you and the phrases, and every time that phrase is heard he will think of you.

Observer-Expectancy Effect

People are much like scientists, we are constantly performing tests and experiments. We test each other in order to develop and understanding of one another, and we test our environments to see how we can overcome limitations. As we do so, we formulate some expectations regarding the final result of those tests, and we may formulate these expectations as we engage in the experimentation, or even before we begin.

With an expected outcome in mind, people often unconsciously manipulate the variables of those experiments, or otherwise misinterpret the information that is gathered, so that the outcome better matches those expectations.

Before presenting an idea or conversing about a particular topic, it may make sense to begin by understanding the expectations that a person has and, if necessary, first aim to alter those expectations.

Projection Bias

People often have a natural tendency to believe that others are much like them, or that we are all essentially the same. Perhaps for some brief moments we forget that people are all different. This idea of similarity, of course, changes when additional information about others is made more apparent. The interesting thing is that this effect is likely to reoccur with future encounters, even when we have previous knowledge about the differences in other people. It is as if every time we meet people, we unconsciously project a likeness of ourselves into other people, until that projection is slowly removed through the recognition of differences.

When speaking about other people, their actions and their behaviors, be certain to point out the differences that may have caused those actions and behaviors. This may include past experiences and traditions, learned knowledge, beliefs and values, personality, etc. As an example, "Joe has worked in sales his whole life, so he approaches communication a little differently than most people."

Reactance

As humans, we naturally prefer being in control of our own freedom, and when an attempt to remove or constrain that freedom exists, a fight or flight scenario is created… Just like a lion being cornered in the wild, we fight back!

Reactance occurs when we are told to do something or told not to, or when we feel that our choices are being removed or limited. It can also occur under direct pressure, such as the pressure to accept the views or opinions of other people. This is all subject to our perception of control; if we don't feel threatened, no reactance occurs.

> Don't attempt to remove another's perception of control unnecessarily. Use softening statements and questions where possible, and use alternative questions where limited choices are available. Alternatively, use words and phrases that place you and the other person on an equal level.

Selective Attention & Selective Perception

People are naturally driven toward pleasure and away from pain. In this effect, we tend to selectively ignore those things which cause us emotional discomfort or otherwise go against our values and beliefs. We also give more attention to those things which make us feel good.

> Use words and phrases that make people feel good or evoke positive emotions. Vividly recreate events

in their mind of times when they felt great or of future expectations of feeling great. Help them imagine the sensory input from past, present and future occurrences.

Provoking Memory

We talk about memory as if it is a single thing or area that exists within our minds. Memory is actually a process that occurs throughout many regions of the brain, beginning with sensory input that is processed and 'perceived', and filtered according to differing levels of importance. From there, the brain begins to create a series of neural maps within the brain where groups of neurons (electrical points in the brain) are conditioned to fire in unison.

Unfortunately, our brains don't all process information in the same way. First, the information we receive is perceived differently, and thus filtered differently and processed differently. Just one of those neurons we spoke of could be used for several bits of memory from different events that may or may not even be related. Those neurons may also create crossed lines in the neural map we spoke of, which can cause different memories to begin blending together. Below, we take a look at some of the memory-related issues that can occur and how we may be able to use some of them to our advantage.

The Verbatim Effect

Memories are encoded as representation, imagery, and abstract idea… It is for this reason that people are more likely to remember the idea of what is said, rather than verbatim word for word.

If it is not necessary for the listener to remember what is said word for word, then use generalizations to "paint a picture" in the mind of the listener. Use vivid imagery that activates the five senses and arouses inner emotion.

Repetition Effect

Memory is encoded in repetition… As information is repeated to us, whether by ourselves or by an outside source, the neural maps that encode information within our brain are strengthened, encouraging long-term memory.

Repeat key words and phrases to ensure that they are better encoded into your client's memory.

Spacing Effect

Information is better recalled if exposure to it is repeated over a long span of time rather than a short one.

If you have important information to communicate, consider spreading that information out during a conversation. Provide the information in sections or chunks, and lead the client in and out of normal conversation, pulling their attention in when important information is provided. When repeating information, provide longer intervals between repetitions.

Primacy – Recency Effect

When information is provided in a list or sequence, those items near the end of the list or sequence are the easiest to recall, followed by the items at the beginning of the list or sequence. Items in the middle are the least likely to be remembered.

When providing important information to your client, try to structure your conversation so that the most important things are talked about first or last, and the less important things are provided mid-conversation.

Modality Effect

The modality effect works hand-in-hand with the "Recency Effect". In this, we are more likely to remember the last items of a list when they are received via speech, rather than when they are written.

The Heightened Interest Effect

People tend to remember those in which their interest was elevated or "heightened" at the time of learning it. As our interest is heightened, we become more emotionally charged and our level of alertness increases in regards to the object of interest.

Create a connection between the information that you wish to relay, and the topics that your listeners are interested in, have much knowledge about, or deeply desire.

Self-Generation Effect

Self-generated information is more easily remembered than information which was given to us. For instance, people are better able to recall memories of statements that they have made than similar statements made by others.

Whenever possible, instead of telling people the information that you wish to relay, give them the opportunity to discover that information for themselves. One way of doing this is through the use of questions. Ask them a question (or a series of questions) that directs them to answer, allowing them to provide you with the information you want them to know.

Context Effect

A person's ability to process and remember information is dependent on context. This means that if the information has been used or will be used in a specific context, that information is more likely to be remembered.

Consider or discover specific upcoming situations or contexts in which your client will be engaged in the near future, and create a connection between your message and that context. You will also want to ensure the client recognizes how beneficial your information will be to that specific situation, and (if possible) imagine using your information.

Humor Effect

Humor helps us remember things, possibly, because as we find things humorous, they tend to stick out in minds as they are found more distinctive, or perhaps it is due to the emotional arousal. Either way, humorous items are more easily remembered than items that are not found humorous.

You can use humor in the form of direct jokes or anecdotes, or you can include humor as part of a short story. You can also include the information to be remembered directly into the jokes, anecdotes or stories; or you can provide the information before or afterward, as a metaphor or simile.

Illusion of Truth Effect

People are more likely to identify as true statements those they have previously heard (even if they cannot consciously remember having heard them), regardless of the actual validity of the statement. In other words, a person is more likely to believe a familiar statement than an unfamiliar one.

Misinformation Effect

The misinformation effect is a primary reason for the occurrence of false memories. It occurs when new information skews our perception of previously accepted information. This is most likely to happen when the new information is received immediately after the original information.

Von Restorff Effect

This is also referred to as the "Isolation Effect" or the "bizarre effect". The more something appears to be "different" or "out of the ordinary" the more easily it is likely to be remembered. Our brains are hardwired to learn, and that means paying attention to things that are different and automatically processing those things that are not.

There are many methods of making information appear to "stick out" or be different during conversation. These include any significant alternations in your voice (volume, tonality, ambiance, etc.), repetition of words and phrases, and dramatic appeal (which may include body-language).

Zeigarnik Effect

In the early 1900's, Dr. Bluma Zeigarnik , a Russian psychologist and psychiatrist, performed an extensive series of tests about the need to finish something that has been started, and this is what he found: When a task is uncompleted, it signals a set of alarms in the brain that alerts us of its incompletion. This not only causes us to become more aware of it, but also creates a sense of dissonance that drives to us to see the task through to completion. This is the same feeling we get when we engage in an interesting movie and (for one reason or another) don't get to see the ending. Such an effect also triggers emotional cues such as curiosity, interest, and desire.

> You can draw people in with incomplete phrases. Just like a movie, the more your listener is directly involved in what is being said, the more they will feel drawn in. Break your sentences up, and consider adding additional phrases to prolong the conclusion. Use sentences that begin with "You know...", "You can feel...", "You can see..." (i.e. you know exactly what it's like ... I know you do... To be drawn in by sentences that are incomplete).

Cryptonesia

Often, when people experience something objectively, meaning that there is no emotional element to the experience at all, we may forget having had the experience. Upon remembering the experience without some subjective element to it, we may mistake the memory as imagination.

If you want people to remember what you're saying, begin by ensuring there is a subjective element to the conversation. Raise their emotions and make it personal to them.

Egocentric Bias

People tend to view their own experiences subjectively, and the experiences of others objectively. This plays through in our memory of our experiences also… Egocentric bias occurs when we recall our past experiences and abilities as being better than they were.

This happens with most people and ties in to the self-interest principle, so when people talk about their own experiences, evaluate what is said from an objective viewpoint.

Fading Affect Bias

It's our unconscious mind that drives us toward pleasure and away from pain. We generally tend to hang on to pleasant memories, whilst unpleasant memories fade away more rapidly. The most memorable experiences are generally those that satisfy our deepest emotional needs, and are rarely duplicated.

Bring your clients back in time to moments where they felt great… Many of these moments will be a first time – The first time learning to ride a bicycle, the first prom, that first kiss. Find ways to create connections between these moments and your conversation.

False Memory

This is essentially the opposite of cryptonesia. It occurs when imagination becomes mistaken for memory. False memories may form when social demands are placed on a person to remember, but they are having difficulty doing so, and this can amplified when they are encouraged not to place much thought as to whether or not their constructed memories are real or not. They can occur when the person is being coerced into believing, or even simply accepting mild suggestions (see "misinformation effect"), that an event occurred in a certain manner and some related memory of the event already exists.

Mood Congruent Memory Bias

The way we feel now can be found to affect the way that we remember past situations. Our memory recall tends to make the attributes of past experiences more congruent with our current mood. This means that if we feel happy right now, we are more likely to see past situations in a more positive light; but if we feel unhappy right now, we are more likely to see those past situations more negatively.

If you want someone to remember an experience more positively, ask them to recall that experience when they are in a good mood. Even bad experiences can be remembered as being "not so bad". Conversely, if you want them to remember the experience in an ill-mannered way, get them to recall the experience when they are in a bad mood. You can find ways to stimulate those experiences, such as pre-empting the conversation with another (possibly related) experience or using a combination of verbal and non-verbal cues (see "Anchoring").

Chapter 4

So What Do I Say Now?

*Improve Your Basic
Conversation Skills*

*E*ffective conversation starts with you. You can't always rely on others to have great communication skills, and so if you want to be a great communicator, you have to rely solely on your ability to communicate well, armed with the knowledge that what you say is only as important as how you say it. There are various pre-emptive techniques to assist in your effective communication, including:

Posture & the Effect of Body Language

Every part of the body affects every other part of the body, but also affects the mind, the way we think, and the way in which we perceive and understand the world around us. This book is not intended as a study of body language, and so it will suffice to understand that certain postures are associated with certain emotions and those emotions change our perception.

If, for example, we sit forward in a slump, with our head tilted slightly toward the ground, a common posture when tired or depressed, we are likely to also feel tired or depressed, thus lowering our attentive abilities and purposely ignoring other information, or viewing information in a more negative manner.

On the contrary, if we sit up straight (with the spine erect) with our head up (so that the crown of the head is highest), we automatically become more alert. Relaxing the shoulders and smiling will then give a more positive feeling, and thus we are more likely to view any information positively (see "mood-congruent memory bias" in chapter 3).

Spend some time playing with the way in which posture affects your tonality, emotions, and the impression that you leave on others. For example: An erect posture gives a confident and positive emotion and tone. A slumped posture, gives a negative and depressed emotion and tone. Each of these has its place depending on the impression that you want to leave. From a sales point of view, when talking about your offer, you want to portray positivity. When speaking of competitive offers, you may not.

As you learn about the effects of body language on your conversation / communication, as well as on your emotions, perceptions and cognitive functions, consider how you can cause change in your clients by helping them access their own posture and body language.

Dynamics

Dynamics includes the volume and ambiance at which you speak. The dynamics of your conversation should be appropriate for the audience to which you are speaking. If you are speaking directly to one individual, your conversational dynamics should be appropriate for one-on-one conversation. You may also want to take into account the environment in which the conversation takes place – You wouldn't speak at the same volume in a library as you might in public.

People often change the dynamics of their conversation (along with tone, inflection, and pace) when a change in emotion occurs. Under particular circumstances, you may want to portray such emotional changes to get your point across (without actually being emotional). Consider how such changes may affect your listeners.

Tone

The tone of your voice can say a lot about you. People are always making judgments about others… To decide what type of personality they have, what type of thought process they hold, and what type of mood they're in. Often, this is done simply to know if others are approachable, and if it makes sense to communicate and/or form some kind of relationship with them – even if only temporary.

Over the years, we learn to recognize and associate certain tones with certain demeanors. Think for a moment about an army sergeant speaking to his troops in a training exercise. Even if you've never met an army sergeant in your life, you've probably watched enough movies to know that the sergeant will speak with a low tone of voice, probably with a quick and snapping attitude. Now consider the way in which your grandmother is likely to speak with you. Do you imagine something a little different? What about a husband telling his wife how much he loves her? Can you imagine the tone of voice that he would use?

Before communicating with people, think about the image that you would want to portray and the feelings that your target audience would feel in accordance with your tone of voice. During the conversation, consciously play with the tone of your voice to add dramatic appeal to your conversation according to the emotions that you want to portray and the message that you want to get across.

Inflection

Inflection is the change in tonality that (in most of us) occurs naturally as we speak. Much like tone and dynamics, a change in inflection can be a sign of emotional change. A rising tone can signify excitement, whereas a falling tone can signify seriousness.

> The most effective speakers learn to dramatize their ideas through the use of inflection. Effective use of dramatization can catch the listener's attention, keep their attention, and get them emotionally involved.

String-Ends

A string-end is the end of a sentence or phrase… The last word or words spoken that conclude the sentence or phrase. Intonation used in a string-end generally provides some indication as to the use of the sentence. It is well understood, for example, that rising string-ends (the tone rises at the end of the sentence) are an indication of inquisition (questions). On the other hand, falling string-end (where the intonation falls at the end of a sentence) are an indication of a command. Neutral string-ends are acknowledged as ordinary statements.

> Listen to the string-ends used by others in their conversation. People often try to hide questions they don't want to ask, such as when a statement is made with a rising string-end, which could signify that speaker is unsure of himself. An attempt to conceal a falling string end (hiding the act of commanding) can be an indication of self-control in the face of anger or frustration.

Pace

Pace is essentially the rate of conversation. People generally speak at a pace that corresponds to the way they think. People who speak quickly generally process information faster. This does not necessarily mean they are more intelligent as it gives no clue as to which information they are processing, simply that they are processing information at a faster rate. Often, people who process information more quickly are prone to be forgetful and absent minded.

Conversational rhythm may also be an indication of emotional state. As people become more excited, they tend to speak at a faster rate. As they become depressed, they tend to speak at a slower rate.

People generally compare the pace of others to their own. This is true for conversation, as well as non-verbal communication such as body-language. If your pace is too quick, they may consider you as being sporadic; if your pace is too slow, they may find other associations to derive meaning from. The best practice is to match the pace of your clients. This will ensure that they feel comfortable with you.

Rhythm

Rhythm is directly associated to pace. Rhythm is the pattern in which people speak. People who are speaking in a broken rhythm are generally taking more time to think about what they are going to say next, which can be a good or bad depending on the reason. Common reasons for a broken rhythm in speech are: consideration of the next phrase or sentence; Being lost for words (not knowing what to say next); and Anxiety.

Work toward being able to speak with a strong and secure rhythm, while still pre-thinking the words and phrases that you use.

Speaking with a steady rhythm can cause people to enter into a trance-like state as they listen to you carefully. This is not unlike the state that you can enter when watching television, or listening to music.

Eye Contact

Keeping good eye contact lets the other person know that you are paying attention to them and that you are involved in the conversation at hand. When you do not keep good eye contact, people may be weary of whether or not you are listening to them as they speak, which may cause ill-feelings and resentment toward you. These feelings may never be revealed, but will leave the other person walking away feeling bad (often feeling as if you don't care).

Good eye contact does not mean that you need to stare consistently, but rather frequently. Ensure that you are looking them in the eye, rather than at other areas of the body, and certainly rather than looking away. When people are talking, and they find you looking at other things, they are likely to feel (on some level) ignored, and will consider the distraction that has grabbed your attention to be more important than what they have to say.

Distancing

People generally do not fear conversation with strangers, unless they feel the conversation will bring harm to them in some way – whether it is physically, emotionally, or mentally.   It is for this reason, when engaging in conversation (especially with strangers), that the practice of distancing is so very important. Distancing involves pacing yourself in a position that that allows the other person to perceive the conversation as being safe and free from potential harm. There are several aspects to this:

1) Free from physical harm: If you are physically in the presence of the other person, try to place yourself physically outside of the person's personal barriers. A review of proxemics communication tells us that a person's personal space is generally within 1 to 1.5 meters away from their body.

2) Free from emotional harm: People drive themselves toward those things that make them feel good, and away from those things that make them feel bad. In beginning new conversations, you should aim to make people feel good. Not neutral, not bad… Good! Stray away from making comments that may be perceived as judgmental, ridicule, or distressing. This includes that use of jokes and humor as well as direct comments. I can guarantee that even in well-developed relationships, the use of such humor is still likely to leave an ill-founded mark.

3) Free from mental harm: Here, by mental harm, we are really referring to mental overload. People are not always in a position where they feel like concentrating on unexpected conversation, and often prefer to prepare themselves before doing so. Putting people in a position of mental discomfort or mental stress for which they are unprepared can often appear overbearing, and a feeling of resentment or dislike is the usual result.

To get closer to people – physically or emotionally, you need to gain their trust, build mutual respect and get them to like you. You may also want to consider developing pre-established expectations regarding the relationship and the topics of conversation – for example: If someone feels they can open up to you and talk to you about personal topics right from the start of the relationship, then they are likely to continue feeling this way throughout the relationship. Decide beforehand what types of conversational expectations you want to impose on the relationship.

Purpose & Meaning

The meaning of messages is constantly reviewed throughout this book… Every message you speak should be well thought out. Too many people, taking their spoken language for granted, talk without thinking first and in turn regret much of what they say. Your message should always be deliberate and with purpose. If your message has no purpose, it may be better not to say anything at all.

It is through purpose, that we plan and establish the meaning in our message. This can take one of two forms:

1) Explicit Meaning: Looking at "Speech Act Theory" described in chapter one, explicit meaning can be thought of as the locutionary force. This is the direct meaning that is associated with your message. If you say for example "You're pretty smart!" the explicit meaning would be understood that you are commenting on how smart the person is. It is the literary meaning of the words being spoken.

2) Implicit Meaning: Referring back to our "Speech Act Theory" in chapter one, implicit meaning is a combination of illocutionary force. It is the meaning that is implied through conversation or through of use of the words spoken. For example: The word "blue" may be used to describe someone who is depressed (not necessarily colored blue); or the phrase "on a high horse" may be used to describe someone who thinks highly of himself (and doesn't really mean the person is on a high horse).

Even the simplest messages may be misconceived. You may intend to communicate the explicit meaning, and the receiver may generate an understanding for the implicit (or vice-versa). To be a great communicator, you must first learn to consider how each message may be viewed, both implicitly and explicitly, and if there is room for misunderstanding, be extremely specific, or don't say anything at all (communicating through non-verbal communication alone).

Congruency

Although we touched a bit on congruency earlier, it was deemed necessary to briefly revisit the subject in this chapter.

As you deliberately produce purposeful messages, it is important to structure those messages so that they may be easily understood. Your message must make sense. It must have a structured flow. It is when we talk and do not think first, that we are most likely to generate messages that are viewed as scattered, sporadic, or sense.

Types of Sentences

Before we continue with what to say and how to say it… It is important that we first recognize four distinct types of sentences:

Declarative Sentences

Declarative sentences are designed to state a fact. These are usually (fairly) short sentences that come to a full stop (as if written with a period). Declarative statements may also be:

1) Positive Declarative Statements: These are designed to state a positive fact. This form of sentence will start will phrases such as:

> "It is…" (It is communication that drives relationships).

> "I can…" (You can use this information if you try)

> "These are" (These are powerful bits of information)

2) Negative Declarative Statements: Negative declarative statements are designed to state a negative fact. Examples include:

> "It isn't…" (It isn't hard to evaluate this information)

> "You can't…" (You can't go wrong by applying these techniques)

> "There / Those aren't" (There aren't many who are well skilled in the art of communication)

3) Neutral Declarative Statements: Neutral declarative statements state a fact that is neither positive nor negative.

> "He will be going to the store in an hour"

"The car is red"

"The word keeps turning round and round"

> Declarative statements are often subjective, meaning that they are provided in one person's point of view. Don't be afraid to question declarative statements... Consider asking questions such as "How do you know?" or "Are you sure?" or "How can you be sure?"

Exclamatory Sentence

An exclamatory sentence, also referred to as an exclamation, is a stronger, more forceful version of the declarative sentence. Rather than simply stating a fact, the exclamatory sentence is often used in a defensive manner, and can most often be recognize by the subtle use of a rising string-end (the tone of voice rises slightly at the end of the sentence).

"These are my books!" (Not yours!)

> Exclamatory statements are used when a person feels strongly about something. Make sure that you begin by responding to the emotion involved in the statement. For example: Person A yells "These are my books!" Rather than responding "No they're mine!" Person B responds "I understand that they look like your books, but if you look inside you'll find my writing all over them"

Imperative Sentences

Imperative sentences give a direct command or forceful request. The word "imperative" means "of vital importance". Much like declarative sentences, they are usually short and may be spoken with elevated pitch and volume. Imperative sentences are usually spoken with a falling string-end (the tone of voice lowers at the end of the sentence). Stronger imperative sentences may be found to use modal operators of necessity (must, have to, need to, should).

"You have to read these notes."

Imperative statement may or may not be easily accepted by a recipient, depending on the emotion and intent that is conveyed with them. Consider the following imperative sentences:

"You have to check out this new movie!"

"Go to your room!"

The first is of a persuasive nature, and the second is direct and abrasive.

Be cautious in your use of imperative statements. If perceived as a command, these statements may spark a fight or flight response and cause the recipient to become aggressive.

Interrogative Sentences

The interrogative sentence is used to ask a direct question, or interrogate. It is usually some word in the middle of the sentence that is emphasized with the use of tonality, volume or inflection. NOTE: That the use of indirect questions is actually considered a declarative sentence.

"You've have read these notes" (in a questioning manner)

Spoken with a falling string-end, interrogative sentences may appear as a statement, rather than as a question. Ensure that a rising string end is used. This is a common communicative error; learn to anticipate the intent that is used in other speakers to decipher if they are using an interrogative or declarative statement.

Small Talk – Starting A Conversation

Whether you're starting a conversation with a stranger, or beginning a conversation with a friend or family member that you haven't seen in a while, small talk is the key to getting the conversation started – The first step to building (or re-building) that sense of relationship and familiarity. Below, you'll find the important techniques to engaging in small-talk and getting the conversation started:

Simple Questions

In gaining a person's attention and starting a new conversation, begin by asking simple questions that get the other person involved in the conversation. The first few questions that you ask in sparking conversation are very crucial, because if you ask questions that people can easily answer, they are likely to be glad that you asked; but if you ask questions that they cannot answer, they will resent you for having asked. This is because people have an inherent need to feel good about themselves, and when they do not have answers to questions, they will often feel inadequate and may attempt to avoid the question(s) all together.

A good example of simple questioning is to begin conversation by asking questions about minor matters. Such topics may include: the weather, the news, and other recent events or occurrences. You may also ask simple, non-intrusive personal questions such inquiring about the person's name, inquiring about their current activities (what they are doing), or asking about past experiences that relate to the conversation in some way.

Opinions of a Minor Subject

Most people love sharing their opinions. Ask people "what do you think about...?" If you ask people for their opinions on a topic, do not scrutinize their opinions or condemn them for it, as this will certainly result in resentment and the conversation will come to a close.

When asking a prospect for their opinions, try to rephrase your response to be in agreement with them. The more you agree, the more you further the relationship; conversely, the more you disagree, the more you cause emotional friction in the relationship. If you need to disagree, do so by using statements such as "I can see where you're coming from, and I also think...". Be cautious to use the word "and" rather than "but", as "and" shows you are adding to the conversation while "but" is used as contradiction.

Self-Interest

People are most interested in two things: Themselves... And those things that they are interested in (whatever that may be). When you start a conversation with someone, and begin that conversation by talking about yourself, your experiences and your interest, people are likely to think "So what?", "Why should I care?" or "What does this have to do with me?" They may not speak these thoughts out loud, and they may attempt to be sincerely interested, but it is more likely that, unless the conversation relates to them in some specific way, they will not really be interested.

You can begin a conversation with almost anybody by appealing to self-interest. When sparking a conversation with strangers, I often look for something unique about the person (or at least unique compared to others in the immediate vicinity at the time), or possibly something of interest that they are doing at the time, and begin conversation about that particular thing.

When you appeal to someone's personal self-interest, however, their attentive behavior is elevated as they pay more attention to the conversation at hand. Their listening abilities, as well as their abilities to access memory and retain information are heightened.

Whenever possible, begin conversation with the other person's self-interest. Once you have their attention and interest, create connection between their self-interest and the topic that you wish to speak about.

Keeping The Conversation Going

One you have them talking, you may want to keep them talking. By keeping the conversation going you guide the conversation towards matters that you wish to speak about. You can also get people to slowly divulge information to you that may help further the conversation even more, help in further building the relationship, or help you in closing the a deal. Below we discuss ways of keeping the conversation going:

Show Of Interest

It's amazing how people just want to be heard. They just want somebody to listen to them, and they want someone to be interested in what they are

> If You Let People Talk Long Enough, They'll Disclose Their Entire Lives To You.
>
> - *Dan Blaze*

saying. People want to feel important, and they want to feel as if their ideas and what they have to say is important too. You can get through lengthy conversations by simply listening, and showing some interest in what people are saying – This is often referred to as "conversational encouragement". When people believe that you are sincerely interested in what they are saying, they will often continue talking about the topic of the conversation. There are many things you can do to show interest in the conversation, including providing subtle cues such as ummms and ahhhhs and ohhhs, nodding your head in agreement, and possibly looking upward to show that you are processing the information that they are providing. Keeping frequent eye contact is a sure sign of interest, and even simply smiling can show interest.

By appearing interested in what the other person has to say, you gain a level of rapport that says they are important to you, and what they have to say is important… And when you show interest in other people, they will be more likely to show interest in you also.

Opinions Of A Particular Topic

The more involved the conversation begins, the more you can slowly move to more personal areas of interest. Never start a conversation by asking for deep personal opinions. Remember that earlier we spoke about "distancing" - this should be kept in mind until a mutual feeling of comfort has been achieved. However, once a level of comfort has been achieved, you can begin asking for more in depth opinions on particular topics. Again, as noted earlier, do not scrutinize their opinions or condemn them for it, as this will certainly result in resentment and the conversation will come to a close.

You can use funnel questioning (and reverse funnel questioning) to help keep the conversation going on the topic of discussion. With every answer a person provides, you can get them to be increasingly specific about the topic, or otherwise get them to be more and more generalized. Alternatively, you can also run through a list of W-H questions (what, why, when, where, who, and how).

Tell A Story

Since the days of our early childhood, we are all told stories. Good stories provide us a method of communicating interesting facts, sharing abstract principles, and giving important lessons in an engaging way. They captivate us and draw us in, and almost mesmerize us as we imagine the events of the story happening in our own minds. This gives the story a strong sense of reality. Story-telling is discussed in chapter 8.

Stories are very powerful tools for providing explanations and suggestions, conveying ideas and in persuasive communication. Learn to become a master of story-telling.

Progressive Disclosure

Progressive disclosure is about reciprocity. People can often be afraid to share information about themselves, possibly for fear of having that information used against them in some way – But when you begin by sharing information about yourself first, others are more likely to return the favor by sharing information about themselves too. As with reciprocity, you will find that as you share small amounts of information about yourself, others will return the favor by sharing even more information about themselves.

When combined with self-interest (a sincere show of interest in the convention) and progressive questioning (asking minor, non-intrusive questions and slowly asking deeper and deeper questions) this can lead to an astonishing result.

Conversational Hooks

Later, in chapter 6, we will discuss specificity, and the importance of being specific in your conversation. There are, however, times in which being specific is not desirable. Times when it is not to your advantage. Such times may include the use of some persuasive techniques, negotiation techniques, attempts to conceal certain information, and presentation and conversational techniques aimed at generating curiosity. 'Conversational hooks' are such devices.

A 'conversational hook' is device that aims to develop curiosity and (perhaps) interest in other topics of conversation, allowing the conversation itself to flourish into other directions. This is different than the methods used to direct the conversation, in that it does not necessarily control the direction in which the conversation will flow, but rather aims at capturing the client's interest in other topics for the purpose of further prolonging the conversation.

The interesting thing about this method is that it gives the appearance that the client is the one who has decided to move the conversation in the particular direction, so that the client feels he is in control… But what's more, is that it causes the client to use probing questions, thus increasing his investment in the conversation (and possibly in the relationship).

A 'conversational hook' is designed by providing a statement or question, and leaving it in an incomplete status, much like a hook in a presentation where the presentation fulfills the curiosity set forth by the hook. Here, the conversation fulfills that curiosity. You can create a hook by making a statement or asking a question, and leaving it incomplete. Below are some methods of doing this:

1) *Observational Fragment:* Observational fragments are essentially incomplete sentences derived from the observation of something. These sentence fragments will usually start with some form of pronoun, such as "that", "it", "I" or "he". Here are a few examples:

That's really interesting!   I love that!
That's so strange…   It makes me curious…
He's so crazy.

To use these statements as conversational hooks, you must insert them outside of the flow of ordinary conversation. Let's look at one of these for example: "That's really interesting." On its own, this sentence fragment does not give any indication as to what "that" is; however, the context of the situation may give some indication toward this. Still, it does not give any indication as to what it is that is so interesting. This statement is designed to drive a person's curiosity, and force them to ask "What is so interesting?" Once asked, this now allows opportunity to either continue the conversation or move the conversation in a direction involving the new topic.

2) *The Flashback:* The flashback is when you give a glimpse of an event or part of your past, but don't provide all of the details. This can be done when the client does or says something that reminds of such a past event. You disclose a piece of information related to the past event and leave the client with a sense of incompletion or curiosity regarding your comment.

Let's say you and your client were talking about a recent business meeting, and your client says "I think we covered a lot of ground during the meeting" – You could then say "Yes we did, it reminded me of a meeting I once had with my nephew when he first started his business". The client may wonder "<u>How</u> does it remind you of that?" or he could be curious as to "What kind of business does your nephew operate?"

3) *Stating Questions:* Stating a question refers to the act of telling the prospect what he is or should be asking. Some words to start your statement may include:

You've got to ask yourself   You must be wondering
I'm sure you want to know more about
I'll bet you want to know   You're probably curious

Let's review this… Assume you're talking with a client about an upcoming business offer and the prospect refers to a competitive offer. You could reply with, "they're offer sounds pretty good, but you've really got to ask yourself if it's worth it." The ambiguousness of this would cause the client to ask "Is 'what' worth it?"

4) Unresolved Answers: Unresolved answers are used when a person asks you a question. Essentially, you answer the person's question with an elusive or incomplete answer that keeps them curious.

Imagine that you're having a conversation with a client and he asks, "What do you think about the hockey game last week?" You would then respond something similar to, "It's exactly what I expected it to be. What do you think?"

Some common methods of providing unresolved answers include the use of the following phrases:

Just as I thought.	You know how it is
Couldn't be different	It's interesting how that happens
Well… You know	I knew that was going to happen
What do you think?	Can you guess?
I can't believe it	You'd never believe me

The trick, again, is not to provide additional information, causing the person to be even more curious about your response.

5) Partial Answers: When you answer a question, but only provide a part of the total answer, people become curious as to what the remainder of the answer entails.

For example: Let's say you were at a bar, having a drink with a friend and you use an observational fragment "Oh wow…" Your friend then responds with "What is it…" and you reply "I just saw the most amazing woman".

In the case above, you've provided partial informational by stating that it is a woman you've been astounded by, a woman that you just saw and that you thought she was amazing. However, you didn't provide any information as to why she was amazing. Chances are, at this point, your friend will either quickly look around to try to get a glimpse of her, or he will ask "Where! Where!" The adrenalin kicks in and everybody is excited!

6) Metaphorical Representation: This includes the use of metaphors to make a statement or answer a question. These types of answers can be recognized by their use of words such as "It's like…" or "It's as if…"

For example: Say your client asks you if you like the new proposal for an upcoming project, you could respond "Well, it's kind of like that movie – The Italian Job". Here, you would keep silent and await for the client to respond. He'll most likely ask how the proposal relates to that movie. This gives the opportunity for the conversation to flourish by talking about that movie, or movies in general.

Directing The Conversation

There are times when you may want to guide the conversation toward a particular topic. You may want to combine conversation techniques with sales or persuasion techniques, negotiation techniques, inspire and motivate your listener or there may be some other reason. Below you will find a list of techniques for altering the course of conversation:

Conversational Stacking

Stacking is a technique where you stop talking about one thing and start talking about another, without the use of any transition. You simply move through various conversations on various topics until you reach one that resonates with both the client and yourself – one that you both can enjoy talking about. "Stacking forward" refers to simply cutting the conversation on each topic short, usually as soon as a lack of interest has been observed, and moving to a different topic.

Stacking is abrupt as there is no transition between topics, and should be used amongst friends and casual conversation. It is generally best with people whom you have an established relationship with or in remote social settings (such as a bar, a party, etc.)

Controlling Questions

Control questions are questions that attempt to control a person's response or answer to the question. Control questions are typically not really questions all, but rather statements that sound like questions. They are made to sound like questions by use of a rising string-end. The following are examples of a control question "But you do want to buy this new product?" or "This is the right color?"

While controlling questions may be persuasive (by use of coercion), be cautious in using controlling questions as they may be found offensive because they give the impression that you are removing a person's option to choose. A better method is to use a statement with a tag question such as "But

you do want to buy this new product, don't you?
Or "This is the right color, isn't it?

Funnel Questions

Funnel questions allow you to move the conversation from a generalized point of view toward a more specific view, or vice-versa. This can be especially useful in situations where you want to talk more about a specific topic within the original conversation, or when you want to move away from a specific topic of conversation – perhaps to transition to another topic.

You can apply funnel questions by starting from a point of generalization such as "How do you like the weather today?". Once you receive a response (let's assume the responder says "It's beautiful weather"), you then begin to ask more specific questions based on the response they have given, by either focusing in on one topic, or by providing alternative choices to further the conversation. A focused response would then be "What aspect of the weather do you like the most?", while an alternative question response would be "Is it the sunshine, or the cool breeze, that you like the most?". You can continue to ask questions that require more specific answers (or more general answers) until you receive the answer that best suits your needs.

Linking Interests

As you allow conversation to develop and ask questions directed at the self-interest of the other person (their needs, desires and interests), you can sway the conversation by being attentive to areas of commonality between the conversation and the topic that you want to talk about.

1) Acknowledge Commonality

2) Establish Link

3) Redirect The Conversation

You can mention the commonality by use of statements or questions. In essence, you establish a link between the previously held conversation and the topic you wish to talk about.

Conjunctions

Conjunctions are small words used to connect sentences together. They allow us to take two opposite ideas, or seemingly unrelated ideas, and create a connection between the two. It is because we use conjunctions naturally in our every-day conversation, that the use of these small words are often overlooked, thus they bypass our conscious thought processes. Conjunctions include:

And	Or	Nor	But
So	Yet	For	However

> You can use two or three conjunctions in succession to move a conversation from one point to another. For example: You can use the skills you need, <u>but</u> you have to learn them first, <u>and</u> this series of books is the best way to learn.

Baiting

Baiting refers to the use of ambiguity in a method designed to draw people toward a particular topic. Just a like a hook in the water, waiting for the fish to bite, and when there is a tug on the line, you reel it in a little bit more, and then a little bit more, and then finally you reel it in all the way.

Baiting is most often effective with techniques such as funnel questioning, and various forms of conversational hooks (described above). These techniques can be used in combination and can be stacked (one technique used after another, and then again) to drive within the listener, an insatiable curiosity in the topic at hand.

Let's see how this works: Say your friend asks you how the weekend was... You reply with, "It was the most incredible weekend!" [Unresolved answer]. The friend asks, "Why was it so incredible? What happened?" You then answer, "Well... Do you remember the feeling when you went on your very first date? That's what the whole weekend was like for me!" [Metaphorical representation]. "How's that?" the friend will ask... To which you reply, "Well, it was just that her and I, and we had a wonderful time together. I can't wait to see her again." [Partial answer]. By this time, the friend is wondering what woman you are talking about, what made her so special, and possibly what you did together. You could then follow this by giving a more complete answer, before or after the friend asks again.

You can see from the above example how the use of 'baiting' can easily draw the other person into your conversation. When the client asks you more and more questions, they generate a greater sense of curiosity, and thus a sense of interest or a "need to know more". You could have simply said, "I spent the weekend with an amazing woman that I met at the grocery store, and we watched moonlight at the beach all weekend." However, the effect would not have been as dramatic.

The use of baiting requires you to pay special attention to the overall messages that are being sent by the client. Check posture, body-language and other verbal and non-verbal signals for signs of frustration. While baiting can keep the conversation interesting and draw the client in, sometimes the client may not be in the mood for such conversational tactics.

Providing Explanations

The focus in this section on providing explanations is to enhance our ability to explain things in such a way that they can easily be understood by others.

We often encounter situations where we need to explain how something works, or why something has happened, or why one decision is (or should be) made over another. The inability to properly provide such explanations may cause difficulties in furthering the conversation, and may even lead to aggravation if you can't be understood.

Not every person will understand things in the same way, and thus it is often important to change or alter your method of explaining accordingly. Below you will find a few simple techniques to do just that:

Chunking

Explanations are often found to be difficult to digest, especially if the explanation is a lengthy one. Most people find it easier to decode informant that is provided to them in small pieces at a time, allowing them to mentally process each piece of information before then next.

The best method of chunking information is to provide the information is a methodological manner... Sequentially is often the most effective way of doing this (by order in which the sequence of events occur). There are other methods that may be used, such as providing information in the order of priority or importance, spatially, or chronologically. You may also begin by condensing or summarizing the information and then elaborating on each point, or you may begin by generalizing and moving to specifics or vice versa.

> Use grounding techniques with each piece of information that you provide in order to ensure comprehension.

Similarities & Association

Jean Piaget, a Swiss psychologist, proposed that we learn new things in a two-step sequence: First by "assimilation", this is where we seek to classify new information based on previously learned information. Next is "accommodation", here, we acknowledge distinct differences between two pieces of information, allowing us to associate a different meaning to it.

You can see how, in the assimilation stage, it is the similarities between things that first become important. For example: A child may see a zebra for the first time and call it a horse… It is not until the dissimilarities are pointed out or recognized that the child puts the zebra into a mental category of its own.

> You can help people comprehend things easier if you first show them the similarities and/or associations between things, and then review the differences.

Generalizations & Specifics

Humans have an inherent need to classify things into groups or categories… This is because we learn new information based on prior knowledge, or "what is already known". Much like similarities and associations, you can use generalizations to help people classify things into a broad category, and follow-up by showing the specifics and differentiations. For example: If you wanted to teach a child what is a dove, you can begin by saying "Most winged creatures are birds" and following-up with "So a dove is a bird, but it has certain features that distinguish it from others…"

Analogies

Analogies also work like associations… An analogy is essentially a comparison between

> "Life is like a box of chocolates… You never know what you're gonna get".
> – *From the movie "Forest Gump".*

two things that are related in some way. Analogies typically use words that show similarity such as:

Like…	As…	As if…
Compared to…	Similar to…	Is to…

Analogies are most effective when accompanied by a short description or elaboration on the similarities that exist... Sample analogies include the use of phrases such as:

"Learning these skills is like riding a bike…Once you learn, you'll never forget."

"Good conversation is similar to living in a dream… It flows from the creative side of the mind."

You can develop your own analogies by referencing the relationship between two separate elements and promoting the way in which those elements are similar.

1) Synonymous Words: Words that have the same or similar meaning (i.e. Open is to close as near is to far).

2) Descriptive Adjectives: The use of words that describe a noun (i.e. as blue as the sky).

3) Connectedness: Show similarities between the way in which things connect (i.e. the cup needs a lid like a house needs a roof).

4) Completeness: Show the connectedness between two parts or incomplete sections compared to two whole or complete sections (i.e. a single thought is like a pebble in the sand).

5) Categorical Class: Describe how something fits into a particular class. (i.e. People, just like any other animal, have primal instincts).

6) Function: Explain the comparison of how two things work. (i.e. as like the sound of silence can sooth the heart, the right words can soothe the soul).

A complete analogy would be to help the listener comprehend the similarity between two things, one of which is simple to understand and may be something they relate to. For example:

> "The road to success is like learning to ride a bicycle, when you fall, you just get up and try again!"

Stories

Stories may be used as a means of providing analogies. Stories are especially powerful for analogy when they involve some type of real-life event that can be directly associated to the current scenario. Keep your stories short so that the listener's attention span is not exceeded and so that the relevance to the current scenario can be easily associated.

As elaboration… If I wanted to explain the value of choosing quality products, I could tell a story about a childhood experience where a bicycle was purchased based on lower price and continuously required maintenance. I could extend the story by adding how a quality bicycle was later purchased and needed very little maintenance. I would then provide a link to the current scenario by showing how the same choice in quality applies to everything we purchase.

Interrupting

Interruption is an effective way to redirect conversation to whatever topic you want. You may wish to focus on something that was already suggested in the conversation, or you may wish to redirect the conversation to a new topic. It is generally understood, however, that interrupting others while they speak is considered rude and unprofessional – It is for this reason, that methods of interruption should be used to allow the interruption to appear less abrupt, and more pleasant.

Agreement Interruption

It would be easier for someone to get upset with you for interrupting in disagreement, or for what may seem to be no good reason at all... But interrupting for the purpose of agreeing with them seems to be more acceptable.

When using agreement as an interruption technique, two forms of continuation are recommended:

1) Direct Continuation: You can continue the conversation by directly following the agreement statement with any information related to the original conversation itself.

2) Use of Conjunctions: You can create a "linking interest" by using conjunctions, allowing you to direct the conversation according found commonalities in the linking interest.

Use of Conjunction

While conjunctions may he used after an agreement interruption, you may also consider using conjunctions as direct interruptions, such as: "So what you're saying is..."; "But I also think..." or "And that is why..."

Using Their Name

Studies have shown that the use of a person's name in conversation causes them to stop, acquit their thought patterns, and become highly attentive. This is so powerful in fact, that police officials are trained to use a criminal's first name to cause them to stop running when they attempt to flee the scene.

Using a person's name often in a conversation can help to retain their attention. However, be cautious not to over-use their name. If you want to retain people's attention in a conversation, you should use multiple methods of doing so. I find that in a lengthy conversation I use a person's name once at the beginning of the conversation and once (perhaps twice) in the middle of the conversation.

Interrupting with Questions

Asking questions is a common sign of interest in the conversation. It is perceivably difficult (but not impossible) for someone to become upset or irritated for being interrupted when the reason for interruption is simply learn more about what they have to say.

Don't just interrupt people with a question, but find the right moment to interrupt. Wait for momentary breaks in the person's speech pattern.

Interrupting With Permission

Probably the most polite, professional, and respectful manner of interrupting is to ask permission! When you are given permission to interrupt, you can then direct the conversation in any manner you wish, and it is difficult for the other person to mind, as they have already given you permission to interrupt.

This is, by far, the best method of interruption. Asking permission to interrupt someone is a sign of respect, and leaves the impression that what you are about to say is important.

Non-Verbal Cues

The use of non-verbal cues can also be a good method of interruption. Non-verbal cues can include body-language, facial gestures, as well as sounds such as uhhuh, ohhhh, yeah, mmmmm, and so on. You may also consider using non-verbal cues in combination with other methods of interruption.

Making Statements

Before you begin to look at techniques used in making statements, I would strongly recommend reviewing the "Types of Sentences" as described earlier in this chapter.

> Better to remain silent and be thought a fool than to speak and to remove all doubt.
> - *Abraham Lincoln*

When making statements, if you want to avoid conflicts, it is important think of how the other person will receive what is being said. How will they perceive your words and your intention? How will that perception make them feel? How do your actions, your body language, and the situational context relate to what is being said? How are they likely to reply?

I know what you're thinking; I thought the same think once… Gee that seems like a lot of work just to make a simple statement! Remember in chapter one we said that the human brain processes billions of bits of information per second – Once trained; it is capable of processing all of this information in a split second. Even better, once adapted it becomes habitual, meaning that it becomes an unconscious automatic process. Below are some techniques that you may have already adopted:

Euphemism

Some words, although technically the right words for the situation, give an undesirable or unwanted impression. To change the impression or mental image associated with our words and phrases, we may use euphemism. Euphemism is a figure of speech where the invasive expressions are substituted for expressions that may be considered less invasive or more 'politically correct'. For example:

Instead of using the phrase "he dies", we would say "he passed away".

Instead of using the phrase "You're fired", managers use the phrase "You've been let go".

Other common euphemisms include: A little off; bath tissue; battle fatigue; challenged; correctional facility; expecting; gone south; he's lost; kick the bucket; leave the room; politically incorrect; play a losing hand; private parts; rest room; reverse engineering; senior citizen; shell shock, take legal action... And there are many, many more.

Conversational Hedging

Hedging, in conversation or linguistics, is a term that refers to the insertion of words (usually adjectives and adverbs) whose purpose is to lessen or soften the impact of the overall phrase. This may be done to appear less direct or forceful, or it may be done to provide a sense of uncertainty.

The idea of hedging in conversation may have originated from euphemism, as they are essentially similar in nature, except that euphemism is restricted to words and phrases that are deemed "harsh", or undesirable; while hedging is used in a more general sense.

"There are a few <u>minor</u> problems we need to address."

"<u>It's up to you</u>, but you might want to change careers."

"When you speak arrogantly, it's <u>kind of</u> rude."

Sorry, I didn't feel there was any explanation needed here!

Conversational Repair

Communication between two or more individuals often results in misunderstanding or non-understanding, as we have discussed in chapter 2. Thus, Conversational repair is used by the speaker to change or alter what is said; or by the listener to make such a request. This generally happens when either a speaker makes a mistake in his speech, or the listener does not (fully) understand the message that is being conveyed. There are four main facets of conversational repair:

Repetition

Repetition, as it would appear, is the act of repeating all (complete repetition) or part (partial repetition) of a sentence in order to ensure understanding.

1) Keyword: The repetition of a sentence emphasizing a particular word of importance.

2) Key Phrase: The repetition of a phrase that holds some significance or misunderstanding.

3) Recycling: recycling is the act of repeating something that has previously been said, but rather than repeating a previous statement in its entirety, it is shortened (meaning some parts may be deleted or left out) for the sake of ensuring the basic understanding.

4) Re-Ordering: reordering is simply the changing of the syntax – the order that words are spoken, so as to put the words in a preferred order. This is usually only done when a slip of tongue occurs and words are spoken in the wrong order.

> "It's that I just... <u>It's just that I</u> wanted to ask you something important"

* The use of verbal rapport strategies as discussed in chapter 5 are very important here.

Insertion

Insertion includes a host of techniques where additional information is inserted into the sentence.

1) Clarification: Clarification happens when additional information is provided in order to make a statement less confusing or more understandable (i.e. I took a train downtown today, <u>a subway train</u>).

2) Elaboration: Elaboration is the process of taking a simple statement, and such as "I like that car" and providing ample information as related to the statement, often using the word "because".

> "I like that car because when I was a kid my parents had an older version of the same car and it was a great car to ride in, but it also brings back all those old memories."

3) *Addition:* Repeating what was said, but adding additional or more specific information.

4) *Definition:* Here, we take a word or phrase that might appear vague or unrecognizable to the listener, and provide a definition for it prior to continuing on with the remainder of the sentence.

5) *Expansion:* Expanding one original sentence into two separate sentences.

6) *Explanation:* Explaining specific terms used in the sentence.

7) *Parenthesis:* Parenthesis occurs when we insert additional information directly after a spoken utterance, thus causing a break in the sentence, before continuing on with the sentence itself.

Substitution

Substitution occurs when we substitute one word, sentence or phrase for another, generally without adding information or changing the overall meaning of the utterance.

1) *Revision:* This is the use of alternative words, phrases, or sentence structure (syntax).

2) *Replacing:* Replacing occurs when the listener has not fully accepted what was said, and a repletion is made replacing an original word or phrase with a new one.

3) *Word Searches:* Word searches occur when we begin a sentence and become indecisive as to what to say next. This could occur because of internal or external influences, for example, we may simply lose track of our thought process, or the context of the conversation may in some way change, causing the former intentions to become inappropriate.

Deletion

Deletion occurs when we stop mid-sentence, and, without completing that sentence, move on to another sentence, thus ignoring what was going to be said and saying something else instead.

1) Simplification: Simplifying a sentence using simpler or more common words.

2) Alterations: This is the deletion of one phrase for a more appropriate phrase. The second (more appropriate) phrase may provide better clarification, or it may simply seem more suitable under the given context.

3) Inappropriateness: Providing unrelated speech; no response; or discontinued speech.

4) Extraction: Extraction is when you pull one element of a phrase out, deleting the remainder of the sentence in favor of focusing on that particular element.

Active Listening

The subject of active listening has been a topic of interest to communication specialists. In order to define exactly what active listening is, some have developed models of progressive structure that provide a step-by-step guide to listening actively. Of those, three popular models include the Four-Step Model, the SIER model and the HEAR model.

Combined Models of Active Listening

There are many theories and models on effective listening, and many of them cover the same attributes. Rather than cover them all in this book, which I believe would be very repetitive, I have attempted below to combine the most predominant theories in order to give you a more complete overview of the listening process:

1) Hearing: hearing is the process by which we acknowledge auditory input. Acknowledging input does not necessarily mean that we attend to it. You can hear someone speaking without listening to a single word they say, just as you can hear the sound of traffic on a busy street without paying attention to where the sound is coming from. Hearing, therefore, is only one step in the active listening process.

2) Attending: Attending, often referred to as "sensing" is the process of being attentive. In the attentive state you raise your awareness of both visual and audible stimuli. You will want to ensure that you are being receptive to both verbal and non-verbal cues in order to gain a good grasp on the whole message.

3) Understanding: Understanding is primarily about interpreting, evaluating and associating meaning to what you've heard that was accepted in the attending phase. This is not a skill that should be taken lightly, and may take practice… Learn to make better judgments in your interpretations and evaluations of words/sentences, non-verbal cues and the emotions of others.

4) Remembering: Remembering is about storing information in order to provide a response. What you do or don't remember is affected by what you are attentive to, as well as well as your listening intent.

5) *Responding:* Finally, in active listening, we must show that we have comprehended the message by responding accordingly. The response does not need to be verbal, and simply smiling or nodding your head is often a sufficient enough response. In some cases, a response is not necessary, such as a classroom lecture, however, in one-to-one conversations, it is best to provide an appropriate response when possible.

Dramatic & Subtle Variation

Much like shifts in posture and non-verbal gestures, people's moods, emotions and/or thoughts, either consciously or unconsciously, tend to create variations in vocalization (described earlier in this chapter). Those changes may occur in regards to the conversation, the context / situation or in terms of you personally. Great listeners will learn to recognize shifts or variations in a person's conversation, not only in the words they use, but also in the way in which those words are delivered.

There are two types of variations to look for. Dramatic variations are usually caused by major influxes in emotion. However, these variations may or may not be manufactured. By this, I mean that the variations in vocalization may be generated due to actual emotional changes, or they may be forced by the speaker to give the appearance of an emotional change (possibly so that a purposeful dramatic effect may be created).

Subtle variations in vocalization are rarely manufactured on purpose. They are usually the result of emotional changes being suppressed. The speaker may feel the on come of such emotions and attempt to prevent them from becoming obvious. Some of the variations to listen for include:

1) Dynamics: During ordinary conversation, people tend to speak with a constant level of dynamics (volume and ambiance). An increase in dynamics often means an increase in outward emotions, such as confidence, sadness, assertiveness and anger, resulting in a stronger stance [see chapter 1].

2) Tone: Like dynamics, people tend to speak with a constant tonality under normal circumstances. Changes in tonality occur when either commands are given (the tone goes down); or when questions are asked (the tone goes up).

3) Inflection: Variations in inflection are very important; as the meaning of a phrase can be altered dramatically through changes in inflection [see 'inflection' earlier in this chapter]. Changes in inflection can also be signaled by emotional variances. This is very important for anybody who works in sales because these variances could signify a buying motive, or the activation of decision triggers (ideas that influence the change in a person's decisions)… These changes in inflection are often accompanied by words and utterances such as "I see", "really!", "wow", "ohhh", "mmm…" and so on.

4) Pace: Change in pace means generally means a change in thought process… When speech occurs at a faster or more upbeat pace, it usually signifies a rise in expressive emotions (such as happiness, excitement, anger, etc.). When speech occurs at a slower pace, however, it may either be associated with suppressive emotions (such as sorrow, sadness, guilt, doubt, etc.) or it may be due to an increase in the processing of logic (a decrease in emotion).

5) Rhythm: When rhythm is consistent, it is generally because the person's thought process is being taken care of mostly by the autonomic portion of brain – meaning there is little cognitive thinking involved in conversation – This could be due to the ease of the topic of conversation, or it could be due to the use of preconditioned responses (the person has memorized what to say under certain circumstances).

On the other hand, when a higher degree of cognitive thinking is involved in the conversation, the rhythm to which a person speaks will become less consistent (possibly even "broken"), as additional time is required to think of what to say, or to respond to questions.

You use a person's rhythm to your advantage to move them toward a particular direction of conversation (simply keep the conversation going and slowly increase the emotional component of the conversation).

You also can cause changes in habitual behavior by breaking a person's rhythm – Thus forcing them to restart their thinking patterns as they stop and re-analyze the situation. This can be done by introducing something that appears out of the ordinary into the conversation. For example: If your client is going on a tantrum about topic, you can change their rhythm by making emphasized statements like "Hey, look at that over there!"

Chapter 5

Building Verbal Rapport

Make More Friends Through Language

$\mathcal{R}$apport is what happens when there is mutual understanding and when there is a degree of emotional resonance that exists, and perhaps even a feeling of personal synchrony. Below, we discuss several methods of establishing emotional resonance, and increasing rapport.

Use Their Name

We are conditioned to unconsciously believe that those people who use our name, more specifically our first name, must be people whom we know. After all, strangers don't just call us by our first name if they don't know us... strangers would call us Mr. "_X_" or Mrs. "_Y_".

Emotional Resonance

Emotional resonance exists when there is a feeling of commonality between two communicators. Let me repeat... a FEELING of commonality. When two people in a conversation appear to have enough in common that they feel comfortable engaging deeper and deeper in conversation with each other, there is emotional resonance.

Conversely, emotional dissonance (also referred to as "emotional friction") occurs when a person feels uncomfortable in conversation with another person. They may even feel uncomfortable simply being in the same vicinity as the person who has caused the emotional dissonance.

If your goal is to engage in satisfying conversations, and I'm sure it is..., then it's important to understand what things cause emotional resonance, and which can cause emotional dissonance. After all, we (as humans) are all truly emotional creatures, and emotion will most often override our sense of logic and understanding. Dale Carnegie, in his book: "How To Win Friends And Influence People", provides a great understanding of the causes of emotional resonance (of course, I don't believe he actually uses the term "emotional resonance" in his book).

The short of it is, when you make people feel good – both in terms of themselves and in terms of the relationship, you create emotional resonance. When you make people feel bad, you create emotional dissonance. When you do not make people feel either good or bad, you do neither. The trick is to think about how people will feel about each phrase, before you say it.

> In every conversation, you should attempt to gain both mutual understanding and emotional resonance.

Vocalization

To build good rapport through conversation, it is important to adhere to the standards, schemas and expectations of the listener. In basic terms, you need to be the kind of person others would want to build rapport with. It is therefore important to remember when communicating with others, regardless of whether that communication is verbal, written or non-verbal, that people are always making judgments about you, whether consciously or unconsciously. It is for this reason that is important to be cautious of the words you use, as well as the way in which words are used. You want to ensure that you are sending the right message through the totality of your conversation. Under some circumstances, you may also want to take advantage of the fact that you know they will be making such judgments about you – and they always do. Below we review some common perceptions about the manner in which communicators speak:

Pace

As noted earlier, people generally speak at a pace that corresponds to the way they think. Unfortunately, people generally perceive fast-speaking individuals as more intelligent; and slow-speaking individuals as less intelligent. It is also perceived by most, however, that people who speak too fast are emotional, erratic or even crazy – there is a fine medium somewhere, and nobody knows exactly where that is.

Proper Pronunciation

Correct pronunciation is a standard for intelligence. Most people would like to consider them intelligent beings, and as such want to have business relationships in an intelligent manner with other intelligent beings, regardless of the emotional content of a conversation. If you can't pronounce your words properly, the prospect will have some doubt as to your level of intelligence and thus also the level of intelligence behind your offer.

Vocal Sturdiness

It is a natural tendency to speak with a "shaky" or unsteady voice when scared. The problem is that when the prospect on the telephone hears you speak with an unsteady voice, they too understand that you're scared, but don't usually associate that with the simple fear of conversation. Simply put, the prospect will quickly and unconsciously evaluate reasons why you would be scared, and the most common reasons are understood as:

1) Fear of deception being uncovered: There are many scams occurring throughout the world today, and the prospect will consider whether or not you are trying to commit a scam.

2) Lack of confidence: People speak with an unstable (or "shaky") voice not only when they are unconfident in themselves, but also when they are not confident in what they are saying, in their product/service, in their company, in their promise or guarantee, or generally in their offer in any way.

Volume and Voice Ambience

People with confidence speak out loud and give a feeling of power behind their voice, and their words. On the contrary, people with less confidence will tend to speak in a low and shallow voice. When portraying confidence through volume and ambience, be careful not to overdo it, as any overabundance of confidence can come across as being pompous and over-bearing; or possibly even arrogant.

Stutters

Stutters are often perceived much in the same as vocal sturdiness. When you stutter a lot, people become curious as to whether or not you know what you're talking about, whether you're confident in what you are saying, or whether you are trying to hide something by not disclosing all of the information. If you are on the phone, they may think you're reading from a script. Some may also think of constant stutters as an indication of your level of intelligence. If you have a stuttering problem that is out of your control, it may take several conversations for people to take note of that.

Intonation

Intonation is a direct result of emotion... Without emotion people would probably speak monotonously – like robots. People who naturally speak with little intonation are said to be dull and boring individuals, while those who speak with consistently high degrees of intonation are thought of as eccentric.

Inner-Emotion

Emotions, such as joy, anger, sadness, fatigue and doubt will come across in your conversations, and the listener will recognize them in your voice. The sheer sound of your voice and the way you use your sentences will change depending on your facial position as well as your body posture. These are mostly universal among all people, and thus easily recognized by your listener.

All professionals play the part of an actor - Regardless of your true emotions, you need to portray to the listener that you are happy and eager to be conversing with them. .

Sentence Organization

The level to which your sentences are well organized will also be a factor. When you start

> All the world's a stage, and all the men and women merely players.
> - *William Shakespeare*

your second sentence half way through the first, or provide a series of ideas that are all unrelated, the prospect will believe you are "whishy-washy" or otherwise don't really know what you are talking about. People expect a conversation to flow in an organized manner. And when it doesn't, they have trouble keeping up, and will eventually stop listening and lose interest. Take a brief pause before you begin to speak, to organize your thoughts; and if required, take several pauses during your speech, allowing you to organize your thoughts, and allowing the prospect to digest smaller bits of information at a time.

By mirroring and matching the client's vocalization, you can ensure that any judgment they hold against you will be favorable – because they will evaluate you as similar to themselves. Sometimes, however, rather than matching and mirroring, you may want to portray qualities that are more favorable, both through your vocalization, as well as your body language.

Verbal Rapport

People are all different! In conversation, we speak differently, we respond differently, and we process communication input differently. This is largely because we all have different personalities, experiences, and a different understanding of the world around us. And while we all recognize this is true, we are also quick to judge, and often even criticize others who are dissimilar from ourselves.

You can gain verbal rapport through conversation by first showing that you care enough about the conversation (and about the other person's input) to ensure that you properly understand what is said; and second by using a similar communication style as the person you are attempting to build rapport with, to show that you are very similar to them. You will find several notes regarding this throughout this chapter, and throughout this book. Below, I've provided methods of building rapport through verbal style:

Mirroring (Conversational)

Mirroring means to copy, exactly, what the other person does or says, including their pace, tone, inflection and verbal style.

Matching

Matching means to perform some movement simultaneously or with a slight delay, every time the other person performs a certain action. It is the repetition of two matching actions that consistently happen in line with each other that reach the unconscious mind. Verbally, you can.

Paraphrasing

Paraphrasing means to rephrase what another person has said in your own words, intently reflecting the meaning behind what was said. It is useful when the other person's words are not clear or when there may be more than one meaning to the words spoken and is usually followed by some type of confirmation of what has been said.

Parroting

Parroting is similar to mirroring. Parroting is to directly repeat what the other person has said, but not necessarily with the same pace, tone or inflection. Parroting is often used to question the other person's intent or meaning and is generally used with a rising tone at the end of the sentence.

Word Reflection

People tend to use certain words more often than others, sometimes as a habit and sometimes more consciously. In either case, whether consciously or unconsciously, those words have a particular meaning to that individual. By restructuring your own sentences to incorporate those same words under similar context, the other person will register your use of their verbiage.   Make sure that you fully understand the context or meaning behind the use of the words, otherwise you may appear somewhat foolish to the other person.

Reflecting Verbal Style

Verbal styles are often significant of a person's interests, employment or personality. This not only includes industry-specific words but the way in which words are used together to form sentences.

Extrapolating

Extrapolating means to consider the coming or future effects of what the other person has just said. This shows that you understand what was said by showing that you understand what the outcome(s) would be. You can conclude your extrapolation by questioning or asking them to confirm your understanding of the outcome

Encapsulating

Also called summarizing or recapping, this is when you repeat everything that the client has said in a shortened form (a summary). Summarizing their conversation in this way helps to ensure that you have understood what they have said

Echoing

Echoing is similar to parroting, except that only the last word spoken by the client is repeated.

Grounding

Grounding, or 'conversational grounding', is the process of letting the other person know that you heard his message, and that the message was understood. It creates a sense of mutual understanding as far as the conversation is concerned. Since conversation occurs in a reciprocal fashion [see chapter 1], there is much room for grounding to occur, even if it is not deemed necessary. There are five basic continuers for grounding that are commonly understood. These are:

1) Continued Attention: This includes a list of non-verbal signs and signals, such as nodding of the head, smiling / frowning, or making any gesture that can be understood as referring to what has been said.

2) Simple Acknowledgement: This includes words and phrases that show a sentence has been acknowledged and understood. Such may include: Yes, definitely, no way, sure, I see, etc.

3) Back-Channeling: In chapter 4 we discussed the use of non-verbal cues that may be used as methods of appropriate interruption. Those same non-verbal cues - uhhuh, ohhhh, yeah, mmmmm, and so on – may be used for grounding a conversation. The term back-channeling implies that two channels of communication are occurring simultaneously (the second, of course, being the use of minor non-verbal cues).

4) Interjection: When a speaker pauses, or leaves a sentence unfinished, a responder may "fill in the blank", or otherwise input the missing information to show that he understands what the speaker had meant to say. See the example below…

Person A: "I'm hungry and uh…"

Person B: "You want to go for Pizza!"

Person A: "Yeah… Exactly!"

Some caution must be taken as interposing information into someone else's conversation may be considered rude (it is essentially a form of interruption). However, if this is performed with appropriate timing, it can be a great display of understanding, and everybody wants to be understood… This, in turn, can aid in creating high levels of rapport. There is, however, also the risk of interjecting information that is viewed as incorrect, which could result in a loss of rapport".

5) Clarification: *Clarification can occur in two forms:*

a) Clarifying Questions: These are questions designed to make a request for clarifying statements.

b) Clarifying Statements: These are statements that provide additional information that either provide additional descriptive information (adverbs and adjectives), or otherwise answer one or several 'WH questions' (who, what, when, where, why, and how). Either speaker or responder may make use of clarifying questions. For example:

Person A: "My colleague and I went for a drink at the new clubhouse"

Person B: "Yeah."

Person A: "You know, the one by train house."

* The above was an example of the speaker using clarifying statements. Below, we look at the same situation, where the responder uses clarifying statements.

Person A: "My colleague and I went for a drink at the new clubhouse"

Person B: "You mean the one by the train house"

Person A: "Yeah"

6) Alternative Descriptions: *In conversation, people normally speak with one description of a noun or verb (a thing or an action). Grounding by alternative description means to provide some other meaning associated to that noun or verb, usually either through generalization, specificity. For example:*

Person A: "Do you like flowers?"

Person B: "You mean like roses?"

7) Referential Installments: A referential installment is a method in which the speaker (not the listener) proactively grounds the conversation. It is a method by which the speaker awaits acknowledgement of some specified object or event, before continuing on with a discussion about that object or event. Below is an example of how this works…

Person A: "Do you see the empty bottle on the counter?"

Person B: "yes"

Person A: Can you please put that empty bottle in the recycling bin"

* In the above example, "Peron A" made reference to the empty bottle on the counter, awaited acknowledgement of the empty bottle by the responder "Peron B", and then provided directions to be completed regarding the empty bottle.

Let's look at another example…

Person A: "Did you see that car speeding down the road?"

Person B: "Yeah, that was crazy"

Person A: "I don't know why drivers speed in public zones like that… It leaves a lot of room for accidents."

* *In the above example, "Person A" made reference to the speeding car before continuing on with his views about speeding cars in public zones".*

8) Indicative Gestures: Gestures may also be used to indicate objects or events. Such gestures may occur in real time, or they may be suggestive of objects and events that occur in the past or future. They may include pointing, looking, touching, gestures that suggest shape, etc. Even references to time are often made by either pointing forward with the forefinger, or point over the shoulder with the thumb.

Speaking To Personality

As you appeal to the verbal style of others, you will find a shift in personality occurs as you begin to match their personality more closely. Do this often enough, and you may just begin to forget who you are… Ok, just kidding! The better you understand their personality, the better you are able to use matching and mirroring techniques as described above. It is difficult, however, to completely understand the full personality of each and every individual we meet, and even more difficult to remember those personalities for future reference, and so it makes more sense to group distinguishing features together into groups. There are many theories of personality style that exist, however, the model that I find easiest to work with is the four-type personality styles created by David W. Merrill and Roger H. Reid.

Merrill and Reid classified personality as being in one of four distinct categories. They are:

1) Driver: The driver types tend to be emotionally controlled and often appear to be controlling, knowledgeable, forceful, strong-minded and self-confident. The Driver has clear objectives, which often seem to create a sense of urgency.

Driver-type individuals will respond to timely follow-up, attentive listening, evidence and factual support, and solutions that reflect an understanding of their goals.

This type appreciates those who listen attentively with a goal-oriented focus. When providing a presentation, they prefer results and fact-oriented information with a focus on the outcome.

The Driver tends to respond to stress by becoming autocratic. They want to take control of the situation, and usually feel that they have to do so because no one else has the ability to handle the situation. In confrontations, they exert unwarranted power and may belittle others.

With Driver-type individuals, stick the facts, and ask questions about specifics, actions and results. Communicate objectively, and disagree with facts rather than their opinions.

2) Analytical: Analytical people, just as the name suggests, tend to analyze almost everything. These people tend to be intelligent, organized and efficient with detail-oriented objectives. Analytical people are known for being systematic, well-organized and deliberate.

The analytical types appreciate facts and information presented in a logical manner as documentation of truth. Others may see them at times as being too cautious and overly structured. These types are dependable and very thorough in their work. They generally prefer to keep their distance – emotionally.

This type responds best to a professional and structured approach in which logic and data are provided through factual evidence.

The Analytical, like the amiable, don't like stress, and are likely to do whatever they need to in order to avoid stressful situations. When these situations are unavoidable, they will look for the most logical outcome, without regard for individuals' emotions.

Much like conversation with Drivers, with Analytics you will also want to stick to the facts, but use specifics and don't over-estimate. Discuss the reasoning behind what is said, and use questions that begin with "Why" often. Bring faults and deficiencies up front.

3) Expressive: The expressive types, like the Amiable, are relationship-driven, but often prefer to be the center of attention. They are outgoing and dramatic. These people are emotional and enthusiastic with high energy levels, familiar in dealing with other people, and generally quick to open conversation or communicate. They are also great idea generators, but usually do not have the ability to see the idea through to completion.

Expressive individuals respond best to open and trusting relationships, team-building, and enjoy discussions with good listening and a good line of questioning. They also appreciate being able to provide creative input.

> With the expressive type, you want to build discussions around facts and people (not just facts), giving information in brief segments, and asking questions often. You may also want to summarize often to ensure they have captured all relevant details. Use stories that are short, and fast-moving.

4) Amiable: The amiable type is extremely relationship-driven. As such, they are dependable, loyal and easygoing, and tend to be interactive, personable and cooperative. They like things that are non-threatening and friendly. Amiable individuals generally dislike dealing with impersonal details and cold hard facts, and will take time to establish trusting personal relationships with business associates and also tend to work closely with others to obtain and process information, as well as discover solutions. This type is often described as a warm person who is sensitive to the feelings of others but at the same time is considered to be wishy-washy, flamboyant or eccentric.

This type responds best to cooperation, careful listening and support of each other's personal goals. Provide them with third-party references and guarantees, and perhaps let them assist in the decision making process – this will make them feel close to you. It is because the Amiable doesn't like stress, especially inter-personal conflicts, that they are likely to consent or comply passively with others in stressful situations.

> With the Amiable, you may want to begin conversations by asking about their personal self – interests, family, etc. Appear as helpful and agreeable as possible, and act on joint and common ground. Use personal assurance and specific guarantees and avoid options, probabilities and conversations about risky situations. Show a lot of empathy and exercise much patience.

Conversational Postulate

Conversational Postulate is a term taken from the works of Milton Erickson, a renowned hypnotist; to most, these ideas are known as "softening questions", "softening statements" or "softening the conversation". Conversational Postulate is a term used to define the mannerism of conversation whose intent is to appear less abrupt by simply being nice about things. For example: When sitting at a dinner table and the person next to you asks "Can you pass the salt?", they actually want you to pass the salt, and are not asking about your ability to pass the salt. However, if they had simply said "Pass the salt", this may have been viewed as rude.

Conversational postulate, therefore, includes the use of polite questions that replace direct statements. Below are some examples of what such phrases may include:

Can you…	Would you…	Could you…
Can I…	May I…	Should I…
… If you'd like.	…If you'd rather.	Is it alright if…
If you…	Do you mind…	Would it be…

Using conversational postulate is an important part of removing, eliminating or reducing resistance in your statements or commands. This is because people generally do not like being told what to do, and even if they understand that there is no ill intention behind the statement or command, consciously or unconsciously, it is still processed with abrupt implications.

This concept is very important in business and sales, and for converting statements into suggestions. For example, instead of saying "You need to buy my product now!" you would say "You can buy my product now, if you want to." The second statement creates less emotional friction and reduces resistance to the purchase; while the first statement may have induced the fight or flight syndrome. Even if the client chooses not to move forward with a decision at that moment, the suggestion has been planted. Used in combination with other forms of persuasive language and suggestion, this is much more powerful than an attempt to coerce the client.

Choice Words

Some words create a stronger response than others. This may be due to the meaning or intent that is implied through the use of these words, or it may be because the words evoke some learned social or cultural understanding. There may also be some reactive behaviors that have been learned on an individual basis, and has become an unconscious reaction.

Attention Grabbers

These are words that produce different emotional anchors.

Now...	So...	OK...
Again...	Here...	And...

More Importantly....

Positive Trigger Words (Hot Words)

Positive trigger words, also referred to as simply trigger words or "hot words", are words or phrases that produce emotional anchors. They will be different for every individual; however, some Hot Words will be common for individuals who share a certain personality or characteristic trait. Hot words tend to excite positive emotions very quickly, and drive us to a peak.

Below is a sample of some common "hot words" that are familiar to most people:

1) Bonus: People are attracted to situations where they can get a better value for the same cost. Simply hearing phrases such as "As a bonus…" or "You'll also get a bonus…" causes people to perk up and pay attention.

2) Secret: People like to feel special, and one way of feeling special is to know something that no-body else knows… To have the insider information.

3) Win Big: Much like the feeling of getting bonus, the feeling of winning something is one of gain, and emotional pride in having "won". The word "big" afterward augments the idea of winning dramatically. The use of these words with positive or absolute denotation can create anticipation in the listener.

4) *Dream:* Everybody has dreams. Some aspire to those dreams. When you talk to people about their dreams, you activate deep desires within them that allow passion to escape.

* In addition to the few common hot words above, people may also have hot words that are more specific to them. Hot words are often related to specific situations that surround a person's life. For example: A new born mother would be very sensitive to the word "baby"; a new home owner would be sensitive the word "home"; and a new business owner would be sensitive to the words "increase revenue" and possibly "business growth".

Take some time to make a list of all the "hot words" that are relevant to your clients, and (in the right circumstance) use these hot words as part of your conversation.

Negative Trigger Words

The opposite of hot words, these are words that cause some form of negative response in people, due to their meaning or implication. They create negative emotional anchors in people, and are generally common across different types of people. However, they may be more powerful for individuals who share a certain personality or characteristic trait. Let's take a look at some of these:

1) *Lose:* Most people are afraid of loss. People are generally more afraid of losing something than they are willing to gain the same amount. For example: Would you spend $100 now for the possibility of gaining $200 next week? What if I told you that you were guaranteed to turn $100 today into $200 next week? What if I showed you proof? Would you up the risk to $500? How about $1000? The thought of losing something is very strong in most of us. Words such as "Spend" or "cost" have a similar effect.

2) Regret: People hate to do things they will later regret. Not only does this give the feeling of loss, but also one that comes with lowered self-esteem and guilt.

3) Wrong: People generally like to believe that they are good. Very few people grow up wanting to be bad in nature, so when you tell someone that something is "wrong", "not right" or that some behavior is "bad behavior", most people will search for some inner meaning for which they can redefine the action in question. Phrases / questions such as "Don't do that, that's wrong!"; "How could you do that?' or "I can't believe you would do that' all give the implication that some action is "wrong".

4) Hard Work: If you are anything like me, as soon as you hear the words "hard work" you begin to feel tired, exhausted or perhaps even stressed. Yet, truth be told, I work harder than most people I know. The notion of working hard, however, causes me to think about working harder than I already do. This is amplified when these words are preceded by words such as "really" (really hard work) or "very" (very hard work).

Intensifiers

An intensifier is a word that modifies or emphasizes another word. They change the meaning of other words so as to alter its emotional definition. Essentially, Intensifiers are adverbs that show a degree of something. We use them in everyday language, often without consciously being aware that we are doing so. You may be shooting yourself in the foot when you want to discuss something important and conversationally use words that make the topic appear not important at all.

Some intensifiers are used as defense mechanisms when we want to make something important appear less important, for example: "Don't get mad, I was ONLY five minutes late!"

There are two major degrees of intensifiers according to Randolph Quirk et al (Sidney Greenbaum, Geoffrey Leech, & Jan Svartvik) as first published by Longman publishing of London England (i.e. Longman Dictionary and Longman School of Business) – the two major degrees of intensifiers are Amplifiers and Downtowners.

Amplifiers

Amplifiers are designed to make things appear greater. There are two types of amplifiers. They are:

1) Maximizers: These adverbs modify another word to the highest possible degree. They include words such as:

Completely	Absolutely	Perfectly
Totally	Utterly	Entirely
Fully	Outright	Wholly
Definitely	Exactly	Unquestionably

2) Boosters: Boosters bring the modified word to a high degree, without being at the highest possible degree. They include words such as:

Extremely	Purely	Highly
Very	So	Too
Definitely	Greatly	Intensely
Enormously	Exceedingly	Awfully

Example: The fire completely destroyed everything.

Downtoners

Downtoners are used to modify words to a lower degree. There are four types of downtoners. They are:

1) Approximators: Approximators are words used to show proximity. They include words such as:

Almost	Quite	Nearly
Closely	Just	About
Approximately	Close to	Roughly
Virtually	Practically	Approaching

2) Compromisers: Compromisers attempt to see 'both sides of the coin' or 'both sides of a story'. They include words such as:

More or less	Rather	Kind of
Equally	Comparatively	Fair
Equitably	Evenly	Similarly
Impartial		

Example: BNC: The Queen could concede that with inflation being rather different from what was anticipated in 1990, there needs to be certain adjustments.

3) Diminishers: Diminishers express a lower end of a scale, and include words such as:

Almost	Nearly	Practically
Slightly	Roughly	Close to

Just about   Not quite

4) *Minimizers:* Minimizers express the lowest end of a scale. They include words such as:

Only   Barely   Just
But   Merely   Simply
Hardly   Basically

The most common types of intensifiers are maximizers and minimizers. Use these words strategically to amplify or downplay the meaning of things, or the perception given. These tactics are used in sales and marketing all the time. For instance: "Buy now, for ONLY $19.99" or "Learning to use this stuff will "COMPLETELY" change your life!"

Power Phrases

Power phrases are those that incite some type of specific action, emotion, or thought process from the listener. They are designed to influence and persuade the listener toward those specific actions, emotions and thoughts.

Agreement Phrases

Agreement phrases are intended to promote agreement between yourself and another person. There are several ideas behind the use of agreement phrases: First, by showing that you are in agreement with someone, or that they are in agreement with you, you are in fact promoting similarity and likeness, thus developing rapport. Second, the promotion of agreement eliminates emotional friction – the more you are in agreement with someone, and they with you, the less negative emotions can come into play. Third, the use of agreement provides an opportunity to strengthen the emotional involvement in that topic of conversation, especially powerful when combined with accelerating pace (verbally and non-verbally) and a rising tonality of voice.

Some common agreement phrases are:

"I'm sure you'll agree that…"

"I know you'll agree that…"

"If you're anything like me…"

"We seem to be like-minded individuals, as such…"

"Great minds think alike".

You can also use positive interruption techniques to achieve the same results, such as

"Absolutely, and…"

"I agree completely…"

"Yes, and…"

Character Phrases

Character phrases are a method of behavior labeling: When you set a standard of character for someone, they are generally likely to act in a manner that is consistent with that set standard because no-one likes to feel that they let others down especially if they perceive that the other person views them in a preferable way. This is especially true if you perceivably place people up on a pedestal (so to speak).

Some examples of character phrases may be:

"If I'm reading you right…"

"Intelligent people like yourself…

"You seem to be a very kind individual…"

To take our example one step further, we'll use some of these in context: "Intelligent people like yourself, john, make smart decisions… Do you think that is the right thing to do?" Another example would be: "You seem to a very kind individual, John, can I ask you to do me a kind favor and take a look at my proposal?"

Common Phrases

Common phrases are those that are heard in society, culture, and family. They may have, at one time, been a catchphrase (described below). These phrases have often been around for a long time and because of this, it is likely that most of us have heard them. They evoke feelings of commonality and often drive us to remember the day when they were first heard. Below are a few examples:

"Look before you leap"

"If you don't ask, you'll never know"

"Look both ways before you cross the street"

"Money is the root of all evil"

"An apple a day keeps the doctor away"

Catch Phrases

Catch phrases often come from popular culture: Music, movies, TV shows, media, etc. They are typically associated with some famous person, and take part in driving popular culture. Below is a short list of popular catchphrases.

"Here's looking at you kid" *(spoken by the character Humphrey Bogart in the movie, Cassablanca).*

"Where's the beef?" *(Spoken by Clara Peller in the Wendy's Hamburger Commercials).*

"Same bat time, same bat channel" *(from the batman television cartoon series).*

"I'll be back" *(Spoken by the Arnold Scharzenegger in the movie, The Terminator).*

Preparatory Induction

Preparatory induction is used prior to asking a series of questions. Often, when asked multiple questions successively, people become irritated and/or annoyed, often feeling pressured or distressed, and as a result may either attempt to deceive the questioner or simply leave the conversation all together. The following are methods of easing the listener into the series of questions.

Prefacing

Prefacing is a preliminary statement or question designed to introduce something else (the most common prefacing techniques use questions). It's about softening a statement by introducing it first. The statement or question will often ask for the listener's permission or acceptance of the statement that is to follow. Some examples of prefacing could include:

"May I ask you a question?"

"Could you please tell me?"

"Can you explain…?"

"It would be helpful to know…"

"I need to understand…"

Linking

Linking involves referring to a previous statement or question, prior to asking your main question. The use of "linking" involves beginning a phrase with statements such as:

"You had mentioned earlier…"

"I remember you had said…"

You can also create linking effects by using questions, for example:

"Didn't you say that…?

"When you said… Did you mean…?

"Wasn't it you that mentioned…?

Chapter 6

Specificity

Understand How Being Specific Can Make You A Better Communicator

*O*ne of the biggest issues in human communication is the lack of specificity – the existence of ambiguity, or non-specific communication. Because people are not specific in their communication with others, errors in the communication process occur. Almost all social communication is ambiguous to some degree.

When we communicate with others, we speak in terms of thoughts or ideas that are communicated through representational systems such as images, signs and symbols. The mind goes through a process in which those images, signs and symbols are constructed for each idea we wish to convey, however, in the communication process, we tend to omit certain details, and core concepts regarding those representations. This could be because communication of the core ideas requires us to search within ourselves for the specific ideas generated by the unconscious, and this requires additional time and effort, which may not be viewed as necessary or worthwhile under common circumstances.

The funniest thing happens when a lack of specificity exists: The receiver of the communication (the listener) will usually, rather than ask for clarification, simply replace the unknown with his own information or understanding of the representation. In simple terms, he will fill in the blanks (most likely out of fear of appearing stupid).

The problem is enhanced when lack of specificity becomes habit, or when all communication circumstances are viewed as equal, whether consciously or not. People tend to speak naturally in most circumstances, and do not normally pre-consider the words or sentences they choose.

Another reason for the lack of specificity is that people are inherently lazy. Our brains are designed to filter out what's unimportant, and focus on what is important... and the deciding factor is usually based on an attempt to achieve more with less. Thus we aim to say only as much as we need to in order to get our point across.

> Simply being aware of possible areas of misunderstanding can help make you a better communicator.

Syntactic & Semantic Ambiguity

Dr. Milton Erickson defined three main communication errors that result in a lack of specificity – Deletions, Distortion and Generalizations. But, before we get to that, let's take a look at linguistic classes of ambiguity.

Syntactic Ambiguity

Syntactic ambiguity occurs when a sentence can be misinterpreted as having more than one meaning, mainly occurring from the relation of the words within the sentence.

Syntactic ambiguities most often occur because of the way that words are cross-referenced. Take a look at the following example:

"The woman played with the child in the green shirt." (Is it the woman who is wearing the green, or the child who is wearing the green shirt?).

Consider another example:

> "Yesterday I saw my wife with another man by the window." (Who was by the window, me, my wife, or the other man?)

Syntactic ambiguities can also occur because of the way that words are grouped together. Consider the following statement:

> "Please give me the red and green balls."

This may be understood as "Please give me the balls that are dual-colored – red and green" or it may be understood as "Please give me the red ball, and also the green ball" (using singular form) or it may also be understood as "Please hand me the red balls and the green balls (using plurals).

Consider how your phrases or sentences may be understood and/or misinterpreted by the receiver, and if necessary, rephrase your sentences so they may be better understood. You may add additional information, or repeat and rephrase the sentence altogether. Consider also asking for confirmation that your sentences have been understood by the receiver.

Semantic Ambiguity

Often referred to as lexical ambiguity, semantic ambiguity occurs when a sentence can be misinterpreted due to phonological error - When a word within a sentence can have two or more meanings, thus causing the entire sentence to appear ambiguous. The most common semantic ambiguities occur from the use of:

a) Homonyms: Words that are spelled the same and sound the same but have different meaning. Example: "I saw her duck". (Did she bend down to avoid being hit by something, or did she have a pet duck?).

> **Rumack:** Can you fly this plane, and land it?
> **Ted Striker:** Surely you can't be serious.
> **Rumack:** I am serious... and don't call me Shirley.
> *- From the movie Airplane*

b) Homophones: Words that are spelled differently but sound the same, and have different meaning. Example: "This edition is great!" which may be understood as a new version (edition) or an added element (addition).

Semantic ambiguity can also occur due to the use of slang or industry jargon. For example:

> "The chopper flew right by us" (the word "chopper" is often used to refer to both a motorcycle and a helicopter. Note: that the word "flew" is also a semantic ambiguity and is often used to refer to flight, or in slang it refers to moving at a fast pace).

Semantic ambiguity can also occur due to the use of slang or industry jargon. For example:

> "The chopper flew right by us" (the word "chopper" is often used to refer to both a motorcycle and a helicopter. Note: that the word "flew" is also a semantic ambiguity and is often used to refer to flight, or in slang it refers to moving at a fast pace).

Another example would be:

> "I have to go to the can" (the term "can" could refer to a metal cylinder used to store drinks or it could refer to a toilet).

Other semantic phonological ambiguities may occur within multiple words, compound words, or words that include a prefix or suffix… Consider for example the following: "Incapable hands". Spoken aloud this may be understood as it is written, or it may be understood as "In capable hands"...

Another example would be the phrase:

"He's seeing a psychotherapist" (Is he seeing a doctor who gets you to relax and discuss your problems while he listens? Or is he seeing a psycho therapist – a doctor who attempts to cure cases of insanity?)

As with syntactic ambiguities, consider clarifying your language by adding additional information or rephrasing your sentences to ensure that you are well understood. With compound words and words that include a prefix or suffix, you may consider adding strategic pauses to ensure the listener does not misunderstand the break-up of words.

Synonymous Terminology

Very similar to syntactic ambiguity is the lack of common terminology. Much like earlier examples ("chopper", "flew" and "can" as used in semantic ambiguity), other definitions may be used to describe a single noun or verb. The construction industry for example, uses the same word to describe a sheet of wood known as OSB (oriented strand board), which may also referred to as "particle board", "sheathing" (such as wall sheathing), "sterling board", "aspenite", or "smart ply". This host of available terms used to describe one thing can often make it difficult to understand each other. Terminology may also be different in differing regions, cultures, or social classes.

While it is quite impossible for every person to memorize the entire thesaurus, it possible to apply greater effort to establishing a common term for words when questionable doubt arises.

When in doubt as to the meaning of words, rather than make assumptions, ask questions that begin with "Did you mean…?" or "Are you referring to…?" Don't be afraid to let people know that you are not certain of their terminology.

Deletions

Deletion occurs when we leave out pieces of information. As we communicate, we naturally filter out pieces of information that are deemed irrelevant, unimportant (under the circumstance) or uninteresting, which are all subject to interpretation. This means that what may be irrelevant to you may not be to someone else.

Unspecified Nouns

Deletion occurs when we leave out pieces of information. As we communicate, we naturally filter out pieces of information that are deemed irrelevant, unimportant (under the circumstance) or uninteresting, which are all subject to interpretation. This means that what may be irrelevant to you may not be to someone else.

Unspecified Nouns

Nouns are "things" – people, places, objects etc. People will often speak of nouns without specifying or even considering the possible variances of that noun that exist. For example: You might buy a new car and simply state

"I'd like to buy a new car".

This does not give any indication as to what kind of car you'd like to buy. It often leaves the listener to attempt to clarify the missing information.

Use sentences that aim to force the speaker into being more specific, such as sentences that begin with either "What specifically…" or "What type of _X_ specifically…"

Unspecified Verbs

Verbs are words that denote action. People use verbs in broad terms, usually because they feel that additional information is unneeded. Take the sentence "he left the building" for example – This does not suggest why he left the building, or even how he left the building, but rather allows the missing information to be assumed by the listener (which may be assumed incorrectly).

> **Doctor:** "Captain, how soon can we land?"
> **Captain:** "I can't tell."
> **Doctor:** "You can tell me. I'm a doctor."
> **Captain:** "No, I mean I'm just not sure."
> **Doctor:** "Well, can't you take a guess?"
> **Captain:** "Well, not for another two hours."
> **Doctor:** "You can't take a guess for another two hours?"
> **Captain:** "No, I mean we can't land for another two hours."
>
> -- *(From the movie, "Airplane")*

Use questions that begin with "How specifically…" or "Why specifically…" to attain additional information.

Unspecified Adjectives

Adjectives are words that describe a noun – They describe size, shape, color, etc. Most adjectives used by people in our daily lives are unspecific. Take for example the following sentence fragments.

"The big dog was barking loudly." (Which big dog?)

"I like the blue car." (What do you like about it?)

"That is a very fancy building." (What is fancy about it?)

> Most unspecified adjectives can be specified through the use of questions that begin with "What specifically…", or by attending to the connected noun and using questions that begin with "specifically which…"

Pronouns

Pronouns are words that are used in place of some nouns. Pronouns are often used to refer to nouns, so that we do not have to constantly state the noun itself… Imagine a conversation where a noun was consistently repeated: "My house is small, my house is a cottage by the beach, and I have friends and family visit me at my house all the time"… The repetition of "my house" can appear quite annoying, thus we replace it with the pronouns "it" and "there": My house is small, it is a cottage by the beach, and I have friends and family visit me there all the time".

With the use of pronouns can arise several issues: The first is that they are often overused, and when this happens their meaning can become obscure – They should be used only to refer to nouns that have previously been mentioned (called a referential index) and/or it when is well understood which noun they refer to.

A second problem with pronouns is the misuse of them, meaning they can be placed incorrectly. Pronouns should refer to the noun that has most recently been mentioned. When a second noun is mentioned, it should first be described, and if referring to a previously mentioned noun it should be restated to ensure clarification. See the following example of misuse: "My mother and my sister went to the store, she purchased many things". In this example, the word "she" should refer to my sister, as this would be the preceding noun. If it was intended to refer to "my mother", then "my mother" should have been restated as follows: "My mother and my sister went to the store, my mother purchased many things".

Finally, pronouns are sometimes used without any reference at all. This missing referential index can act similar to universal quantifiers (see below). An example of this would be "it is believed that humans evolved from apes" – This does not specify who believes this, and allows us to assume that everybody believes this (which would be a fallacy).

While there are many types of pronouns, the following is a short list of the types of pronouns that require special attention when their meaning in unclear.

Woman: "You got a telegram from headquarters today."

Man: "Headquarters? What is it?"

Woman: "It's a big building where generals meet."

-- (From the movie "Airplane")

1) Personal Pronouns

Personal pronouns are used in place of personal nouns. They include:

He	She	They	It
Him	Her	Them	

When personal pronouns are used, and the referential index to which they belong is not clear, use phrases that begin with either "Who specifically…," or in the case of the pronoun "it" use "What specifically…"

2) Demonstrative Pronouns

As the name implies, demonstrative pronouns are designed to demonstrate the existence of something. These include words such as:

This	That	These
Those	Here	There

When pronouns are used in an ambiguous manner, clarify the referential index by asking questions that begin with either "What specifically…" or "Where specifically…"

3) Indefinite Pronouns

The use of indefinite pronouns is a primary source of ambiguity due to being unspecific, and should be used with extreme caution. They include:

Some	Several	Few
Many	One	One of
People	Things	Anyone

| Anything | Each | Either |
| Other | Somebody | Someone |

As example, a sentence such as "Some people believe the world is coming to an end soon" does not provide any indication as to how many people believe this... Essentially, any more than one can be considered "some".

Use questions that begin with "What specifically..." or "Who specifically..."

Comparatives

Comparatives are words or word combinations that express a difference between two things, or compare two things. Comparatives are unspecific in that they do not tell to what degree the difference between two things exists.

There are four primary methods of recognizing comparatives, they are:

1) Use of the word(s) "than", "more than" or "more... than". An example of this could include: "This training is more in-depth than other similar training courses!"

2) Use of the word(s) "more" or "even more". For example: "This will cost a little bit more".

3) Use of the word(s) "less" "less than" or "less... than"

4) Use of words ending in "er". For example, "This is a better one".

When comparatives are used, consider seeking to specify them by questions that begin with "how specifically"; "specifically how much...", or "exactly to what degree...".

Excessiveness

There are several adverbs that denote a degree of excessiveness – The most common of which being the word "too". When we use the word "too" preceding an adjective (example: "too much" or "too little") we are speaking in some form of excessiveness. In essence, "too" is a measurement word that does not directly provide measurement, and it is for this reason that it is considered ambiguous. It has become norm to use statements of excessiveness without providing any indication of specifics, and it is thus the listener's responsibility to make an attempt to clarify the situation.

One method of clarifying such statements is to create a comparison. People often make judgments of one thing by comparing them to something else. Thus, the statement "It's <u>too</u> expensive" may be resolved by "Compared to what?", or other similar questions that seek comparison. Another method would be to directly question the statement by seeking a definition, thus the above statement "It's too expensive" could be answered either with "How much is too expensive?" or by "How much are you willing to spend?".

Below are a few words that denote excessiveness:

Too	Very	Extremely
Incredibly	So (it's so…)	Really (It's really…)

Illusion of Choice

An illusion of choice occurs when you are given a choice between two or more things (usually no more than two or three), but the choices offered do not extend to the full scope of choices available. This creates a limitation where there is no need for limitations.

Illusion of choice can be recognized through the use of the words "either" and "or". For example: "Either A or B can be made available." Another example using the word "or" would be "Would you like A or B." (This is called an alternative choice question in sales).

Such statements or questions are designed to prevent consideration of additional choices. Maybe there is a choice C that we failed to look at. Maybe our options are completely open. Who knows?

> Illusion of choice questions or statements are unspecific because they do not provide all the choices. When you recognize that someone has offered an illusion of choice question or statement, consider the context involved, and what additional options may be present.

Distortions

Distortion occurs in the way that we interpret information, both as the sender of the communication and as the receiver. Essentially, the facts become distorted to mean what we want them to mean, instead of what they truly are, this is highly influenced by such aspects as perception, presuppositions, and other means in which our brains recognizes what we see and hear.

Mind Reading

People often make assumptions about life in order to feel prepared for the future. Sometimes, we make assumptions about the thoughts and intentions of other people, and sometimes we do this without warranted proof. An attempt to make assumptions about the thoughts, feelings or intentions of others is called mind reading – We cannot really read the mind of others, but we sometimes think we can, and believe that our assumptions are the absolute truth.

Mind reading is apparent in statements such as the following, and the inherent thinking that is associated with these types of statements:

"I know what he's thinking!"

"I know how you feel"

"I know what he's going to do next"

Omit mind reading attempts in your own communication. When mind reading is communicated by others, seek clarification by asking questions such as "How do you know?" or "How can you be sure?"

Lost Performatives

A lost performative is when a statement is made about a personal belief, that is presented as an absolute or universal truth. Doing this allows the speaker to remove themselves from being directly associated with the statement. These statements often use generally accepted information, established assumptions or popular beliefs to add to their believability. The following are examples of lost performatives:

"Vitamins are an essential part of any diet."

"You have to dress well to be successful."

"You can't be a good communicator if you don't learn this."

Lost performatives should be questioned to seek reason or authority such as "Why would you say…" or "According to who"

Cause & Effect Statements

Cause and effect statement are used to indicate how one thing leads to another. People often make such statements without directly questioning how or why one thing leads to another - When asked how A leads to B, people may not be able to provide a direct answer.

Examples of cause and effect statements may include:

"It makes me angry when he says stupid things." *(Why does that make you angry?).*

"If you eat healthy you'll lose weight." *(Does this apply to everybody?).*

"Bad judgments cause bad behavior." (Is there anything else that causes bad behavior?).

Cause and effect statements are often accepted by the unconscious because they appear logical. However, if we analyze such statements we are likely to find fallacies and/or limiting beliefs that can be overcome.

Complex Equivalence

A complex equivalence is a statement that suggests how two things are the same, or equivalent to each other; or otherwise suggests that one action has a meaning other than its true meaning.

Often, words that connect two statements to make them appear equivalent are omitted as they are presumed "understood by the listener". Such words may include "that means", "that just means", "obviously", "I can tell", etc.

Examples of complex equivalence include:

"You're not looking at me when I speak, so you're not listening to what I say.) (Do I need to look at you to hear what you're saying?)

"The boss has his door closed – He's planning to fire me." (Does he fire someone every time he closes the door?)

"You're not listening to me – You obviously don't care." (How does lack of focus equate to lack of caring?)

Complex equivalences are often used to create a relationship between two statements that are effectively unrelated. To challenge these, it is important to recognize the relationship between those sentences and directly question them (As in examples 1 and 3 above) or provide a counter-example (using an opposite or contrary situation – As in example 2 above).

Generalizations

Generalization occurs when we speak in terms of groups, categories, or classifications. As humans, we all have the need to label the things in our environments as our brains create maps of our worlds. This is, to one degree or another, different for every individual.

Generalizations may also occur when we take an event or experience that has

> All Things In The Universe Are Dependent On Circumstance
>   - Dan Blaze

occurred in one situation, and apply that event or experience to other situations that appear similar. An example of this would be to say "Children need discipline." This statement does not apply universally... Not all children need discipline, and those that may, would not need discipline all of the time. The need for discipline itself may also be a subjective viewpoint (one's own perspective).

Modal Operators

Modal operators (often called "modal verbs" or simply "modals") are auxiliary verbs, meaning that they add either functional or grammatical meaning to another verb, which simply means they change the meaning or outcome represented by that other verb. Modals precede the verb which they alter, and modify 'how, when, or if' the second verb is performed.

Let's just take a look at a close example to ensure comprehension: Assume I said "I will go to Disney Land". The word "will" is a | modal operator that modifies the meaning of the word "go". This is a completely different sentence then simply stating "I go to Disney Land" (which is an unspecific sentence fragment). Similarly we can replace the word "go" with the word "want" which can also act as a modal operator "I want to go to Disney Land"... In this example, the word "go" does not have the meaning of doing or having done.

The following is a short list of modal operators:

1) *Modal Operators of Necessity*

These are words that denote the necessity of doing something (or not doing something), and are used when there is a belief that something must or must not be done. Perhaps we believe that it must be done a certain way; or at a certain time; or possibly with certain people or at a certain place. This type of language is heard often in statements such as "You have to get a good education to get a good job with a good company" or "You must eat your veggies if you want to be strong". It is possible, however, that such statements of necessity could be made under presumptuous beliefs, thus limiting options that are available to us. These words include:

Must   Mustn't   Have To

 When these words are used, directly question both the reason as well as the authority behind the statement. If no reasoning or authority exists, then question the future outcome by starting questions with "What would happen if…" or "What would prevent you from…" For example:

Statement: You really have to get your act together.

Question Reason: Why must I get my act together?

Question Authority: According to Whom?

Question Future Outcome: What would happen if I didn't?

2) *Modal Operators of Possibility*

Beliefs can be liberated or limited by the boundaries that we set upon ourselves. Often, these boundaries derive from our previous experiences, and/or our understanding of the world around us. The problem is that we often develop or create beliefs that are incorrect, either due to lack of effort in our previous experiences or by applying a context-specific result to other contexts.

To explain this a bit further, consider the following:

a) A student who has previously been good in mathematics takes a university course in business accounting and finds it too difficult. (Previous context-specific results – being good at math – were erroneously applied to business accounting in the belief that they are essentially the same).

b) The same student then states "I can't do accounting" (Previous experience in attempting to do accounting creates a limiting belief about future abilities).

Modal operators of possibility include:

Can	Can't	Could
Couldn't	Possible To	Impossible To

Much like those of necessity, modal operators of possibility can be approached by either directly seeking reason, questioning authority or attending to future outcomes.

> *Statement:* I can't learn all of this!

> *Question Reason:* Why can't you learn all of this?

> *Question Authority:* Who says you can't learn all of this?

> *Question Future Outcome:* What would prevent you from learning all of this?

3) Modal Operators of Judgment

Judgments are in essence decisions, and much like making decisions, people make judgments through a series of mental filters. A person's judgment of something can first go through an assessment of previous experiences, biases, social and moral interpretation, contextual evaluation, and so on. Modal operators of judgment can act much like those of necessity, in that they lead to unwarranted freedoms, or to unnecessary limitations, both of which should be questioned accordingly.

Below is a short list of modal operators of judgment:

Should   Shouldn't   Ought To

Again, modal operators or judgment can be questioned in the same manner as those of necessity or possibility: By questioning reason, authority or future outcome

> *Statement:* You really shouldn't be so sarcastic!

> *Question Reason:* Why shouldn't I be so sarcastic?

> *Question Authority:* According to Whom?

> *Question Future Outcome:* What would happen if I continued to be so sarcastic?

4) Modal Operators of Contingency

People often create self-imposed limitations, or otherwise impose limitations on others, without directly considering what is or is not possible. Below is a short list of these modal operators:

Would   Wouldn't

Modal operators of contingency can be countered by questioning reason or future outcome.

> *Statement:* I wouldn't step outside of my comfort zone.

Question Reason: Why wouldn't you step outside of your comfort zone?

Question Future Outcome 1: What would happen if you did?

Question Future Outcome 2: What would prevent you from stepping outside of your comfort zone?

These modal operators, however, are often used in combination with those of necessity or possibility thus is it also possibly to reply to the appropriate connecting modal:

Statement: I would go to Paris for vacation but I can't.

Question Authority: Who says you can't?

Universal Quantifiers

Universal quantifiers are words that group all things as equal. These are words such as "all", "every" and "always". Universal quantifiers are often used out of context or in situations where they don't actually apply. Consider the following statements for example:

"All of my employees hate me!" (All your employees?)

"Don't mind him, he's always like that!" (Always?)

"She's never happy" (Never?)

When used, universal quantifiers should be directly questioned in search of specifics. One way of doing this is to simply restate the modifier in a questioning tone of voice (as in brackets above). Another method is to question the possibility that opposes the universal quantifier.

Statement: Don't mind him, he's always like that.

Response: So he's never not like that?

A list of universal quantifiers is listed below.

All	Every	Never
Always	Everything	Nothing
Entire	Everyone	No-one
Whole	Everybody	Nobody

To be specific in conversation, it important to omit the use of universal quantifiers, and be able to recognize their use by others.

Chapter 7

Dealing With Difficult People

Communicate Effectively With Difficult Communicators

$\mathcal{T}$his book was not written to provide a course on human behavior; however, there is something to be said about being able to adequately communicate with difficult individuals to achieve a fair outcome. In this chapter, we discuss different types of behavior and review how to hold conversations with individuals who display such behaviors – note that there are many different ways to deal with many different behaviors, here, we discuss only those that promote a healthy conversation aimed at furthering the relationship.

Understanding Behavior

There are some considerations to keep in mind when working with difficult people. First, it is important to understand that all behavior is learned and adaptive. Everything we do as humans is shaped by our experience. When we find something does not work, we discard of it; alternatively, when we find something does work, we use it and may even turn it into a habit. Some of these habits may carry on from childhood to adulthood, or may even become a part of our identity- who we are.

Situational Indifference

To make things a little more complicated, we often fail to differentiate between one context and another. So the same behavior may be used in any situation that has some remote similarity to the original situation in which the behavior was learned.

Behavioral Meaning

All human behavior whether consciously or unconsciously, carries meaning. We act in a certain way because of the meaning that such actions hold (I do this because that is what respectable people do), or because of the outcomes associated with our actions (If I do this, it means that will happen). Such meaning may incorporate our goals, beliefs, judgments, values, morals, ethics, and so on.

Self-Benefit

Aside from meaning, all actions are performed for purpose of benefiting the person acting. Even difficult people act the way they do because, in some shape or form, they feel they will benefit from doing so. The only question is: what type of benefit is it exactly that they are seeking? Some seek a sense of power, some search for a release for their frustrations, some seek to find or avoid consequences, and some people just want to be heard.

Self-Benefit & Positive Intent

If the principle of self-benefit tells us that every action is performed for the purpose of benefiting the person acting in some way; that means that the intent behind every action must have (or have originally had) some positive purpose – this is called positive intent. By first looking for the positive intent behind any action, we can better seek to both define and correct the action. For example, aggressive behavior is most often initiated because of an underlying need for protection (often, protecting beliefs, morals and values), or the need to right some wrong (something that was done to the aggressor that caused him to become aggressive). This being said, if we understand why someone is aggressive, for example, we can then find better ways to deal with their anger or frustrations.

The Golden Rules of Conflict

In all situations involving difficult people, there are a series of restraints that must be applied for proper resolution to occur. These restraints aid in moving the conversation toward a mutual understanding, and apply to all situations, although perhaps for differing reasons:

Self-Control

When working with difficult people, whether they are forceful, aggressive, passive-aggressive, or simply over-emotional, the first step is always to maintain your own self-control. This is not to say that there should be no portrayal of emotion, but any emotion that you portray should be planned and performed consciously, as opposed to being a natural state. If you think you will be working with difficult people often, I strongly suggest that you engage in both anger-management courses as well as theatrical courses (which will also help you in the art of persuasion). Along with self-control, you must also hold a great degree of patience. Without patience, you cannot maintain your own self-control.

Objectivity

As you work at keeping your self-control, it is important that you recognize that as you engage in conversation with difficult people, you are in fact placing yourself into a momentary situation of discomfort. That's all it is- a momentary situation of discomfort. Once the conversation comes to a close, the situation will be over with, and you will need to get on with the remainder of your day without letting that situation effect you. At lease, this is how professional conversationalists view such situations.

That being said, difficult conversations should always be viewed as objectively as possible. Remove your own emotions from the situation, and try to understand the entirety of the situation, what is happening, what has happened, what will happen, what is being said, and how the conversation effects all people involved (and you may not be the only two people affected by the outcome of the conversation). Remember that most people will react to you in the same manner that you act toward them.

Understanding

As you practice self-control and patience with an objective view of the situation, it is very important to try to understand each situation from the point of view of the other person. Step into their shoes, if you will. In order to do this you must take as much into account as possible: What you know about their history, their personality under ordinary circumstances, and if / how the current situation may have affected them. By "putting yourself in their shoes" so to speak, it may give you a better understanding of the source of the difficulty. This is, of course, not to say that all behavior is made acceptable by understanding past events, but rather that such an overall understanding can better your ability to resolve the issues at hand, and may even put your own anger or frustration at ease.

Eye-Contact

Frequent eye contact is an important part of communication, and this is especially true when working with difficult people. Eye contact says a few things about you. It suggests you hold a high level of confidence and a sense of dominance. It also suggests that you are listening attentively and are fully engaged in the conversation. A lack of eye contact could suggest the exact opposite. Look away from time to time as you don't want to stare at others which may be perceived as confrontational, but always for a reason (this is where some of those theatrical classes may come into play)… Look away because you're thinking , because you're feeling empathy, because you're remembering, but never look away without a reason – Doing so, suggests that you are losing your position on the topic, your sense of confidence or dominance.

Open-Posture

While this book is not designed to be about body language, I find it extremely important to review the importance of open body posture when working with difficult people. Non-verbal communication is said to compose approximately 55% percent of all messages. People are always making judgments. We do this in our quest for meaning – and where better to associate meaning than in communication or conversation. Open body posture is a sign of openness to communicate and understand; while closed body posture is a sign of distancing yourself, whether that is a refusal to be open-minded and understanding or simply not listening at all.

When we refer to open body posture, we mean not only your main posture (openness of the arms and legs), but also keeping an open stance (don't try to block the other person in), openness of the hands (don't make fists or closed hands), keeping an erect spine and head held at mid-level.

Active Listening

Active listening is an important part of all communication. Active listening means listening actively to what is said, and the meaning behind what is said, and disregarding unimportant distractions

Types of Difficult Behavior

As we discuss the different types of difficult behavior, we will make reference to methods in which they are difficult in verbal conversation. Note, however, that people who portray these difficult behaviors verbally are also likely to portray the same behaviors physically, so some caution must be taken in dealing with these types of behaviors to ensure your own level of safety.

It must also be noted, that behaviors can occur from situational factors or they can be rooted in personality. For example: One may become aggressive momentarily as a result of some situational trigger; or one may be aggressive as a trait of their personality (and thus display aggressive behavior most of the time). Whenever possible, it is important to differentiate which of the two you are dealing with, as this may alter your overall approach.

1) The Aggressive: Aggressive behavior causes or threatens physical or emotional harm to others. There are two types of aggressive individuals. There are those who have learned, possibly from the early days of childhood, to be (or to act) aggressive upon others. This is an emotional disorder referred to as "dispositional aggression" (or "dispositional anger"). These people have been conditioned to believe that circumstances must occur in accordance with their desired outcomes in order to avoid varying forms of personal loss (i.e. loss of finance, loss of time, loss of opportunity, loss of self-respect, etc.). This conditioning may have occurred as a first-hand experience or it may have been learned through family, peers, and social structure or otherwise. Aggression may also be caused by the inability to deal with one's own emotions.

It is because they have been conditioned by such beliefs that they are more difficult to work with, and may be viewed as pushy or even as bullies. Aggressive individuals tend to enjoy being in power, even if their aggressiveness is only temporary. They prefer to be in control, usually seeking to be respected – Even if by fear, and will prey on those who appear weaker than they are. As they recognize their power over an individual, they may begin to feel superior and will re-assert their aggressiveness over that individual under future circumstances. On the other hand, aggressive individuals recognize and respect strong character on an equal level, as long as they are not being overpowered.

There are also those who become aggressive as their emotions are triggered by external circumstance – This could be a particular situation, or it could be something that was done or said [see also "Expectation Violation" in chapter 2]. These are generally short-lived or temporary instances of aggression, and do not reflect the individuals natural personality. People who become aggressive by such triggers usually feel that they are protecting their rights, beliefs or values, and are willing to do anything to do so. They are most often focused on themselves and the violations that have (according to their own perception) been inflicted upon them and lose the capacity to monitor their actions. This violation triggers high-levels of emotional dissonance, and the aggressor results in behavior that is designed to resolve that dissonance – Such a resolution often means forcing the anger outward externally.

In 1988 a management expert by the name of Robert M. Bramson (Ph. D.) identified three uniquely different types of aggressive people:

a) The Sherman Tank: These are the directly aggressive people who come on strong and forceful. They send direct attacks of criticism and arguments. This may be because of a strong sense of righteousness if they feel they have been abused in some way, because they need to prove themselves right (and in turn devalue the rights of others), or because of a strong belief that making others look bad makes them look good.

> Refrain from showing any signs of fear as this will only serve to confirm their sense of power. Refrain from reciprocating the aggressive behavior, as this will only cause a battle for power, and may result in physical violence. Also, don't use commanding words or sentences. If the aggression is only verbal, allow the aggressor to exert his emotion, and remain calm and unemotional, actively listening to the underlying issue. They may need some time to calm down before they begin to speak with sense and rationality. When the aggressor allows a moment of pause, assert yourself mildly, showing respect, and move the conversation toward the future tense with emphasis on cooperation.

b) The Sniper: These are aggressive people who do not directly attack you, but send indirect attacks through the conversation, in the form of "pot-shots", innuendos, teasing or hurtful remarks. Often, these people will combine their hidden aggression with some form of playful act - You may often leave the conversation wondering "what did he mean by that?" They may hold the belief that by making others look bad it makes them look good.

Begin by identifying the behavior aloud, preferably in a one-on-one session (doing so publicly may cause further retaliation and turn them into a Sherman Tank. Follow this by inquiring about the (real) reasoning behind their behavior. Make apologies if necessary, and seek mutual agreement on ways to rectify the cause and prevent future hostility.

Sometimes people act this way purely for a sense of power, as previously mentioned – making themselves look good by making others look bad. Under such situations, you may consider using light humor as a response. This may diffuse their actions and prevent future actions as they realize that their show of power has no effect over you.

c) The Exploder: These are people who seem perfectly fine until finally they explode. These fits often occur as a result of negative emotions that have been held-back or kept under control for a period time, or opinions that have not been previously stated. It is possible that such negative emotions stem from outside influences, and something in the conversation triggers an emotional release. Exploders are more likely to release their emotions where they feel someone will listen, or under circumstances where they no longer care about the consequences of doing so.

Exploders need a few moments to express their anger, but their anger will subside fairly quickly. Often, they just want to be heard, and they don't care by whom. During this emotional phase, they will undoubtedly tell you about the cause of their anger. Once their emotion begins to subside, interrupt respectively, and speak in terms of cooperativeness (apologizing if necessary), changing their frame of mind toward future outcome. Keep their focus on the future and continue to promote cooperativeness if possible.

2) The Passive-Aggressive: Passive aggressive behavior occurs when people are passive in direct communication, but become aggressive in indirect communication. This type of behavior rarely occurs as a result of situational factors, and is usually rooted in one's personality. These are the people who won't say anything to you, but become angry and often exert their anger elsewhere – Possibly by assaulting non-animate objects, or by expressing their anger to other people. In direct communication, the passive aggressive may make indirect statements such as sarcasm, being critical of what is being said, or simply being silent.

Passive aggressive behavior is usually the direct result of some level of anger or frustration combined with the fear of direct conflict. The fear of conflict may result from the fear of the unknown, meaning not knowing how the other person will act; or it could be from a lack of faith in one's own abilities to effectively handle conflictive situations (especially if one wishes to sustain the current nature of the relationship).

Begin all relationships with a sense of openness – Let others know that they can always talk to you about anything. If you notice someone is being passive-aggressive in response to your communication, they may feel over-powered by you. Get them to open up to you – Begin by talking with a softer tone of voice, let them know that you do care, and that effective communication is necessary for the relationship to flourish. Get them to talk about their anger calmly (and not act out their anger with additional frustration). Cooperatively seek a resolution.

Passive aggressive individuals often look for others who allow them to exert their anger. This may either be someone who is weaker or more subdominant than themselves – who makes them feel powerful; or it may be someone who will simply listen to their frustrations.

If you are on the receiving end in conversation with a passive aggressive individual, begin by openly identifying their behavior for what it is – anger / hostility. Show empathy and understanding, yet establish limitations of behavior – Let them know that they cannot take their aggression out on you. Get them to talk about the specifics of the issue at hand. Get them to suggest better ways of dealing with their issue, and then motivate them to take action on those suggestions.

3) The Passive: Passive behavior does not further a healthy relationship. It puts one person in a dominant role while the other person remains passive, and feels they have not release for their emotions. Like the passive-aggressive, this behavior does not commonly occur due to situational factors, and is usually a result of personality. Passiveness is often displayed by consistently agreeable behavior, or through silent behavior.

Passive individuals may suffer from some form of depression or low-self-esteem, which in turn develops into a fear of direct confrontation (even if that confrontation is minimal). If they do not have some emotional outlet for their frustration or anger, it may build up and develop into an explosive outburst (see "the exploder" above).

> Much like the passive-aggressive, it is important to promote a sense of cooperation and openness. Speak to passive individuals with a softer tone of voice so that they do not feel overpowered. Use much patience in getting them to disclose their emotions.

4) The Assertive: Assertive behavior is a step down from aggressive. Assertive individuals are dominant and forceful, this behavior usually results from some sense of righteousness – They either believe that they are right in their stance on some topic of discussion, or that they have been wronged in some way and are attempting to make things right. Assertive people are very confident, in their directness. It is crucial to handle assertive behavior correctly without allowing it to proceed to the next step – Aggression.

> Assertive people often need to let out their frustration, so listen to what they are saying and do not provide immediate feedback (or they will feel as if you are not "really" listening). When they stop, or pause for a lengthy period, provide them with empathy for their feelings and for the situation that has frustrated them. Use apologies if warranted.

Redirect their focus to possible resolutions, and ask questions that engage logical functions such as "What do you think…" or "How can we resolve…" Use language that promotes cooperation and fairness.

5) *The Negativist:* Any negative behavior that is repetitive exists for a reason. People aren't just born negative, it is a choice (although, sometimes an unconscious one). Sometimes, the negativity is an emotional barrier meant to protect them from the world; sometimes, it's a condition. They may be quick to suggest how you should behave according to their view of the world. Negativists can be recognized by the following:

a) Negative misinterpretations – They often interpret much of what is said in a negative point of view. For example: "You look great today" could be interpreted as "You mean I didn't look good yesterday… What was wrong?"

b) A sense of powerlessness – Negativists often feels that that they cannot change things, and there is no sense in trying.

c) Pessimism – A belief that the future is desolate or dismal, and no matter how hard they try, the future will remain desolate or dismal, and "that's just the way it is."

d) Risk Aversion – Negativists usually refrain from situations that they view as risky or uncertain. To a negativist, anything may be viewed as risky, for example: They may be reluctant to share information about themselves that could later be used against them. They may also be quick to suggest what they feel is risky, for instance "Don't swim in deep water because you may drown" or "Don't spend your money on university, you won't get a good job in this economy anyway."

Try to limit the amount of time that you connect with negative people, but when you have to, remember that just like everybody else, negative people want to be understood – Letting them know you understand them may not only strengthen the friendship but may help change their attitude (to some degree).

Don't allow their negativity to be focused, so learn to change topics of conversation with them quickly. Dissipate negative comments by objectifying them (removing the personal aspect) and by generalizing them (possibly by the use of universal quantifiers – all, every, always, never, etc.). Thus when a negative person says "This restaurant is expensive" you reply "all restaurants are expensive".

6) The Chronic Complainer: The chronic complainer is a negativist of a different breed. They see everything that is wrong with their world, but usually don't realize that their behavior is negative. Many of them even see themselves as "realists", or even "perceptively positive" (and they may actually be positive individuals by nature). These individuals may have learned early that this behavior is likely to get them what they want; or it could be that they had (at one point) no other way to release their disapprovals or frustrations. In either case, the behavior has stemmed from their early life and carried on to adulthood.

Their complaints are usually real, at least to them. The real reason, however, that they complain, is to get attention, sympathy or validation / acknowledgement for their feelings. They identify themselves as victims in an unfair or unfortunate world, and often use phrases such as "Things never change", or "Why does this keep happening to me?"

Begin by acknowledging what they are complaining about, and show empathy for their feelings. Any attempt to get them to see the positive side of things will result in a loss in rapport. Instead, after acknowledging their feelings, simply try to change the subject to some other topic. If they continue complaining about the same topic, offer suggestions, but keep those suggestions short and to the point. You may also consider asking questions directed at a change, such as "So what do about that?" or "Is there a way change that?"

7) The Know-It All: Know-it-alls are often fueled by their own sense of intelligence, and usually carry some genuine sense of superiority or grandiosity. They also tend to hold a bias of perception known as Curse of Knowledge (see chapter 3).

These individuals may have some deep sense of insecurity, in which they feel they must display their intelligence to gain the approval of others. It is this same sense of insecurity that often leads to problems in developing close relationships, in specific, a difficulty with intimacy on any level (even amongst friends). In other cases, know-it-alls may even provoke arguments, often beginning out of a sense of "fun" in order to prove their superior intelligence.

Since they seek attention, give them some of the attention that they desire. Listen to what they have to say when it is relevant to the conversation. When it seems that they are going off course with unwarranted information, bring them back to the topic at hand by use of questions (a good question to ask is "How is that relevant to our discussion?").

Defensive Communication

We are all hard-wired to move toward those things that cause us pleasure, and away from those things that cause us pain or discomfort. As such, we often develop communication habits that are designed to protect us from pain or displeasure. As a child, having done something wrong, when asked about it we may lie and say "Wasn't me, I don't know who did it!" because we learned that being guilty of doing wrong means being punished. As adults, we tend to learn rather different strategies.

In 1999 Dr. Jack Gibb PhD. A former President of the Association for Humanistic Psychology, and a member of the American Board of Professional Psychology, developed a concept of defensive and supportive communication he called the Gibb Categories. In this, he outlines the recognizable differences between communication whose aim is to be defensive in nature, and communication aimed at being supportive of other individuals in the group (this also applies to one-to-one communication).

Gibb describes a pair of six types of communicative behavior, each pair being polar opposites. On the left, he lists defensive communicative climate; and on the right, he lists the supportive communicative climate - Behaviors that strive to be supportive in nature. These are as follows:

Defensive	Supportive
Evaluative	Descriptive
Controlling	Problem-Oriented
Strategic	Spontaneity
Neutrality	Empathy
Superiority	Equality
Certainty	Provisionalism

Evaluative / Descriptive

Evaluative communication is that of finding blame or fault; seeking judgments about things, events or people; or attempts to decipher why something has happened.

Descriptive communication occurs from seeking answers to "what" and "how", as oppose to "why" and "who" Instead of asking questions like "who did that?" [Evaluative], we seek to find out "what happened", "how did that happen?" or "how can we prevent that from happening again?" [Descriptive].

Controlling / Problem-Oriented

Controlling behavior is that of attempting to manipulate others into performing particular tasks or acting a certain way. This essentially suggests that the listener is, in some way, inadequate.

Rather that portray a controlling behavior, the supportive communicator will display a problem-oriented attitude, using solution-oriented language.

Strategic / Spontaneity

Gibb's notion of strategic communication is that of carefully choosing one's words and/or withholding information so as leave out information that may be used against oneself. This type of communication gives the impression that we have something to hide, or something that we do not wish to reveal.

On the other hand, when a person speaks in a spontaneous manner, it conveys openness and freedom to speak whatever is on one's mind.

Neutrality / Empathy

Neutral communication shows a lack of interest in the listener and his concerns. When a listener hears this type of communication he is likely to become defensive, possibly perceiving this type of speech as personal rejection.

The opposite of neutrality would be a show of empathy for the feelings of others, also conveys a degree of personal respect. When we show that we understand the other person, combined with empathy, and a lack of desire to change the other person or alter their thinking, is most supportive.

Superiority / Equality

Communication of superiority is a show or a fight for power. It results in the "us vs. them" attitude. This may cause feelings of inadequacy in the listener, and if the listener cannot display his own assertiveness, may result in feelings of unimportance or possibly inferiority. A person who displays superiority is telling others that he is not willing share ideas, and does not desire feedback.

When a communicator uses words that suggest equality, both people can easily share ideas with an understanding that their differences such as status, power and wealth, worth, etc. are not important.

Certainty / Provisionalism

Certainty communication is displayed by a lack of open-mindedness. It is the "my way or the highway" attitude that results from a belief of superiority in some way. Much like the above comments on superiority, this type of communicative attitude makes the listener feel unimportant or inferiority

A person who displays provisional attitudes is willing to investigate possibilities openly.

Defense Mechanisms

In addition to behavior, attitudes, and personality, are situational communicative habits. Of these, it may be worth a moment to take a look at defense mechanisms. Defense mechanisms are habitual behaviors that are rooted deep within the unconscious, that help defend against situations of conflict or discomfort. When we know something will be uncomfortable to deal with, we use these behaviors to deal with it. The following are a list of defense mechanisms most relevant to conversation:

Avoidance

This is just what the name implies. When we fear a person or situation may cause us discomfort, we may avoid it in order to prevent the discomfort. The problem with avoidance is that the issue never gets dealt with, and may become worse as time goes on. This is especially important in the development of relationships, where a small matter not dealt with today, could cost the entire relationship tomorrow.

> Since people who use avoidance are acting on some form of fear or anxiety of encountering situations they don't feel they can handle, reassure them that things will be alright, and use cooperative language such as "let's", "we", "together", etc. The same applies even if you are the target of the avoidant behavior.

Denial

Denial occurs when we refuse to accept or acknowledge something that is uncomfortable to us. The object of our discomfort is treated as if it simply doesn't exist. Often, when people are in a state of denial, they will also show signs of anger when asked about the situation they are denying. Denial may also be accompanied by other defense mechanisms.

A more covert example of denial, is when we acknowledge a situation, but refuses to acknowledge it for what it is. For example: A business associate loses a deal with a big client who turns to the competition; and the business associate continues to think "I'll just keep sending them offers, and sooner or later they'll come around".

> Denial is an unconscious response to a subjective viewpoint we don't wish to acknowledge. It is thus important to review the situation from an objective viewpoint.

Focus on the things that were ignored and analyze them a little more carefully.

Displacement:

Displacement is a defense mechanism where anger or aggression is projected toward another target, often another person. This is done because the "other target" is perceived as less threatening than the source that caused the anger or aggression.

This is a defense mechanism that occurs often in most of us, we may be angry at another person or perhaps a situation, and displace that anger toward someone that we're talking to. Often, the anger arises when asked about the situation. While displacement of anger or aggression is the most popular, any other emotion may be subject to displacement.

If you are the one displacing your anger on someone else, apologize profusely, and tell them why you are angry. Often the other person will be sympathetic with you and forgive your anger. If you encounter displacement of aggression, show empathy, and help the person realize they are expressing their aggression at the wrong person, for example: "I understand your upset, but I am not the one who you are upset at."

Distortion

Distortion occurs when we alter the way things appear in our own minds, so that reality better meets our own needs or expectations. Distortion is very common, we often either over-emphasize the good to make good things sound great; or we make bad things appear "not so bad".

Distortion, again, is the result of a subjective perception. You can near eliminate distortion by attempting to view situations objectively. Ask others questions that lead to logic and objectivity. Get them to clarify their thinking by asking questions such as "What makes you say that?", "How can you be sure?" or "Is there no other possibility?"

Indirection

Indirection is what we do when we want to say something, but feel we must 'hold our tongue' so to speak, or feel we cannot directly say what we want. This may be because what we truly want to say is considered inappropriate by others, or there may be other reasons.

Indirection is tied to "intent" in "speech act theory". If we say something indirectly that is deemed inappropriate, and the person we are speaking with accepts our "intent" as it is intended, than there is an agreement. If, however, the other person does not accept our intent, there exist a plausible opportunity to deny the intent all together – because it was not directly stated. This is common in situations such as sexual com-ons, bribes and threats; but on a lesser degree, any suggestion that may benefit by leaving an "out" or way of negating the original intent (i.e. "oh no, that's not what I meant) can benefit from the use of indirection. Moving forward in an inter- personal relationship, is a prime example.

Learn to use indirection in your own speech, specifically as a means of gauging the current status, and possibilities of, relationships. Learn to recognize the use of indirection, and ask for clarity of intent – Use phrases such as "What exactly did you mean when you said…"

Projection

Projection occurs when we deny the existence of some aspect of ourselves, but see it as a deficiency existing in someone else. For example: We may deny our own lack of effective communication, and see it is as the other person's bad communication or bad listening habits.

> If a person uses projection with you, chances are they have been offended in some way, and feel the need to protect their ego or make themselves feel less inadequate. Use generalization and self-direction techniques to make them feel better about themselves (i.e. "Don't worry about it, everybody makes mistakes, even me!).

Rationalization

Rationalization is the use of (seemingly) intelligent expressions used to create excuses or reason for a situation. The end result is an attempt at reframing the situation to make it appear correct or righteous. Rationalization is often accompanied by the use of words such as: Since, because, the reason, thus, etc. It is the use of reasonable logic that makes rationalization hard to guard against, both in listening to the speech of others, and in your own speech.

> Rationalization is often used when something that is perceived as controversial or socially incorrect is made to appear alright, tolerable, or 'not so bad'. You'll find the logic that is used in justification is not always the best logic, or is only logical to the

speaker. It may be worth reviewing possible options and consequences with the speaker, of course, if no harm is done, it may also be worth leaving him in his rationalization.

Intellectualization

Intellectualization is essentially the rationalization for the more intelligent. It is the formation of an excuse in a logically sound intellectual statement.

People who use intellectualization are usually trying to remove themselves from a situation, both emotionally, and as an object for blame. Use words that promote emotional content, such as "How do you <u>feel</u> about what just happened?" as opposed to "What do you <u>think</u>…"

Trivialization

Often referred to as "minimizing", this is another form of avoidance, but instead of completely avoiding a situation, an attempt is made to make the situation seem less serious or 'not so important''. This can be recognized through the use of words such as "Oh, it's not such a big deal!"; "It's ok, that doesn't matter" etc.

Much like "justification", sometimes the situation surrounding the use of trivialization has no ill-consequences, and in these cases, it may be best to allow trivialization to take precedence. Many times, however, the person using trivialization needs to be `made aware of consequences and plausible options to reduce those consequences.

Additional Techniques

Above we discussed the top 7 types of difficult behaviors and suggestions on furthering conversation with such behaviors. Below, we'll discuss additional techniques to help prevent problems in communication from happening.

Explanations

Difficult people tend to shoot first and ask questions later. That's why, when providing explanations, it is a good idea to provide your reasons before your statements... Instead of telling them what has happened, and then tell them why, give them the "why" first. Instead of telling them about rules or regulations, tell them why those rules or regulations exist first.

If you were to disclose the statement first, you leave more room for the other person to emotionally interrupt, as they do not yet know the reasoning behind the statement – They are likely to take the first opportunity to do so. By first disclosing the reasoning or the "why" that accompanies your statements (and disclosing the statement afterward), you satisfy their curiosity immediately, and they are more likely to listen to the remainder of your statement.

Thus rather than say "I was late today [statement] because my car broke down [reason]" – You would instead say "My car broke down [reason] and that's why I was late [statement]. Rather than say "I didn't get my work done [statement] because my dog ate my notes [reason]" – You would instead say "My dog ate my notes [reason], and thus I wasn't able to complete my homework [statement].

Apologies

It is a good idea to offer apologies when others become angry or upset, however, be cautious as to what specifically you are apologizing for. Never give apologies without including a reason for the apology, as without a given reason you allow the recipient of the apology to assume a reason – And the assumed reason may differ from the intended reason. You may be thinking "I'm sorry that you are in this situation" and the recipient of you apology may assume you are thinking "I'm sorry but I am not willing to do anything for you?" (Which may only server to cause further aggravation). If you are actually fault, then best practice is to openly admit that you are at fault and apologize.

It often helps to apologize regardless of whether or not the fault is yours. The simple act of apologizing (regardless of what you're apologizing for) begins to ease the emotional discomfort that people feel. When you are not at fault, consider apologizing for the situation that people are in, for the feelings that they feel, for the harm or maltreatment that they have endured, etc. Take a look at the examples below:

"I'm really sorry you feel that way, how can I help?"

"I'm sorry this has happened to you?"

If you had to choose whether to provide an apology at the beginning or at the end of your conversation, you would be better to apologize immediately at the start. Beginning your conversation with an apology should immediately begin to put the recipient at ease, as they await a resolution. Immediate apologies also tend to be viewed as more sincere than those offered at the end of a conversation.

Disclosure of Intentions

Disclosure of intentions is best practice regardless of who you are working with, but is especially important with difficult people. When you are performing some task for the purpose of aiding others, let them know up front what you are going to do, and why you are going to do it. Do not simply let others 'wonder' what you are doing or why.

Referencing

Regardless of the type of difficult person that you are working with, never make direct references to a person's behavior, as doing so can cause discomfort, which in turn is likely to result in a fight or flight response. With a flight response the person may simply walk away, however, if a fight response is triggered, the conversation may get ugly. Thus, never use phrases such as "You're being a jerk" or "You're behaving badly"; instead, reference some of the following:

1) Indirectly Reference Behavior: You can indirectly make reference to the behavior itself, without directly including the individual in the reference. Thus instead of saying "You're behaving badly and I won't take it", you can say "That type of behavior is not acceptable." Instead of saying "You're being a jerk." consider saying something such as "That is not professional behavior."

You may also consider asking to provide an opinion of his own behavior... To do so, use questions such as "Do you think that is appropriate behavior?" or "Do you think that is the right way to approach the situation?" Take some caution in doing this, however, where there is no relationship established and/or no pre-established rapport.

2) Reference Situation: Make reference to the situation that the person has encountered; but quickly move the conversation toward change

3) Reference Emotion: Reference the emotions / feelings that the person is experiencing, but do not allow the conversation the dwell on these emotions. The more you focus on a person's emotions, the more powerful those emotions are likely to develop. As soon as possible, try to switch the person's thinking from emotional to logical by asking questions that allow him to aid in solving the situation. Remember, the more logic goes up, the more emotion goes down. An example follows:

"I can understand how you could feel so angry, what do you think we can do to ensure this doesn't happen again?"

Empathy

Everybody wants to be understood, but this is especially true for difficult people as they (usually) feel they have been wronged in some way, or otherwise feel that they are not understood.

Commands

Refrain from using direct commands... Nobody likes being told what to do, and the use of direct commands can only serve to aggravate or anger people. In chapter 6 we discussed "modal operators of necessity" – Words that denote the necessity of doing something, which include "must", "mustn't" and "have to"... These words should not be used when working with difficult people as they may provoke an already negative frame of mind. Instead, ask questions that provoke action. For example: instead of saying "You have to calm down"; say "It would be easier to help you if you remain calm".

Criticism

Remember that establishing rapport with difficult people is just as important as it is with anyone else. It is thus important to refrain from making criticizing or condemning remarks. Consider this throughout the totality of your conversation, in respect to the other person's opinions, decisions, judgments, values, and beliefs.

Avoidance

Sometimes, with some people, there is no way to get through… No way to communicate. Some people just won't listen, they won't engage in logical or civil communication. Sometimes people just need time to re-evaluate the situation on their own, or to reflect on their behavior. Sometimes… The best thing that you can do is to walk away from the situation, and remove yourself from the difficult person. If you find this is the case, let the other person know that you are leaving, and that the discussion may continue at another time, perhaps when they are less emotional.

Chapter 8

Once Upon A Time...

*Learn How Great Stories
Lead To Great Conversation.*

Stories offer a progression of ideas that momentarily allow the listener to follow along on a journey, taking them away from the world, their worries or problems, and lifting them into another time and place. From the earliest days of our childhood we learn to enjoy stories. They draw us in, capture our imagination, and make us feel involved in the narrated events. Stories are shared through a myriad of mediums, such as movies, games (especially video games), books, and conversations; often shared and handed down from one person to another, or from generation to generation.

When we listen to stories we naturally allow ourselves to relax and slowly drift into a semi-conscious state of mind. If we listen long enough, we may begin to immerse ourselves into the story. As a speaker, you will notice when your listener's reach this state as their shoulders will drop and their eyes may begin to stare deeply into space. It is here that the listener will be most easily influenced, as the consciousness offers little resistance to suggestion.

Stories Types

You can choose different types of stories in order to achieve different results. Consider first the outcome that you wish to attain and secondly, the audience that you will be telling your story to. There are essentially six types of stories from which all other forms of story-telling stem from. They are:

Myths

Myths are legendary stories. They may have originally been created by ancient folk to explain the unexplainable such as life, death, the creation of the universe, and possibly even the supernatural. Myths are mostly based on imagination (or so it would seem) as there is no proof to these types of stories usually involving some form of imaginary characters or creatures. Examples may include heroes, dragons, unicorns, elves, monsters, fairies, gods, etc.

Sagas

The word 'saga' was originally used for any story featuring heroic deeds of a medieval Norwegian hero. Gradually, it came to mean a long eventful narrative about a family, social group, or dynasty with several chapters, cantos, or even volumes. A saga has several legends of heroes added to it and these heroes may be real or half-real (exaggerated truths) as they tend to be based on (at least partially) some real story or event.

Fables

A fable is a short story that teaches a moral point using animals and plants that act human. Acting human could consist of talking (a human language), walking like humans (upright), and other things of that nature. Fables provide lessons and guidance that are very practical and useful in everyday life and thus should be acknowledged for the moral point they provide.

Parables

A parable is a short story that teaches a moral point. It describes a setting, explains the action that occurs there, and highlights the results. The Bible is full of parables along with other religious texts.

Folklore

Folklore are the tales and stories handed down orally from generation to generation, and any real documentation of the tale no longer exists. They generally depict the emotional states (such as hopes and fears) of ordinary people (usually in the local area). Almost every social group has its own folklore traditions and beliefs

Fairytales

Fairytales are usually magical stories of some type of fantasy characters such as dwarves, elves, fairies, giants, gnomes, goblins, mermaids, trolls, or witches. Children tend to enjoy fairy-tales very much because of enchantment and magical power such stories hold.

Preempting The Story

You want to draw the listener into your story before the story begins. You want to have their full attention. By the time you start your story, you want to have begun mesmerizing them, pulling them into another world where the restrictions that they create and the walls they build no longer exist. You want to create an atmosphere where they can feel at ease, engaged, and relaxed. To do this, we preempt the story with phrases that let the listener know we are about to tell them a story, and since most conversational stories are about some past event, preemptive phrases will most often begin with some reference to the past. The following is a short list of such phrases that are recognized as story starters:

1) Let me tell you a story about…

1) Let me tell you a story…

"Let me tell you a story about the time I had to learn the toughest lesson of my life…"

2) Would you like to hear a story about…?

"Would you like to hear a story about the most dangerous adventure anybody's ever had? It all began with…"

3) It was…

"It was only 2 years ago when I was in a very similar situation…"

4) Once…

"Once, I had all he courage in the world but now…"

5) There was a time…

"There was a time I thought I had all the answers…"

6) A long time ago…

"A long time ago, I was searching for answers to…"

7) When I was….

"When I was 17, I learned a very important lesson. I was in the middle of great tragedy when…"

8) I had a friend once…

"I had a friend once, who told me the secret to life itself…"

9) …But before I tell about that, let me tell you about…

"I want to tell you how to improve our performance in just once step but before I tell you that, let me tell you about a time when I was learning to cope with…"

Not only can the above examples be combined;

"It was… Once… Along time ago… When I was young… I had a friend who…"

But they can also be applied with variations:

"A long time ago" could be altered to "long long ago"

"I had a friend once" could be altered to "I knew someone once".

Story Structure

People prefer to receive information in a structured and organized way which helps them follow along, and stories are no different. Through the years, story tellers have developed generalizations of structure designed to make story telling easier. Some of these have divided story-telling into two separate acts, 3-acts, 4-acts, 5-acts and onwards all the way to 22 acts or more! Here, the goal is to provide story-structure that can easily be utilized within general conversation, and so we will stick to the 3-act, 4-act and 5e-act structure:

3-Act Story

The 3-Act story outlines a beginning, middle, and end. It is probably the simplest story structure.

1) Separation: In this part either characters are separated from each other (usually with the main character leaving home), or objects are separated from their owners. In psychoanalysis, we split off uncomfortable, bad objects, often projecting them onto others. In rites of passage, the person leaves their community often symbolically wearing different clothes or markings. In business change, the targets are unfrozen from their current position, readying them for change.

2) Transition: This is often the main part of the story but lasts longer than the climax in a 5-Act structure. The main character (and often other characters) go through some type of change, transition or alteration, usually in the form of trials or hardships.

3) Reintegration: In this part, life returns back to the way it was, often keeping the changes that have occurred in the transition of the story. Characters that have left home may return now return or objects are returned to their rightful owner making things 'normal' again.

* You may consider adding trigger events that help the story take a turn. For example:

You may add a trigger event that helps the story move from separation to transition and another trigger event that helps the story move into the reintegration phase.

The 3-act structure is best used when you want to provide short stories that are quick and powerful (lasting anywhere from 3 seconds to 3 minutes). They are best used with parables, stories of past experience (yours or someone else's), and stories of future predictions.

4-Act Story

There have been many variations on the four-act structure, but the basic essentials are as follows:

1) The Set-up: This phase sets the stage and introduces the key elements of the story.

2) The Problem: A problem is introduced that must be resolved.

3) Deepening the Problem: The state of the problem is amplified so that it becomes a major issue.

4) The Solution/Resolution: A solution is provided that resolves the problem.

The 5 Act Story Structure

Also known as Freytag's pyramid, the 5-Act story structure organizes stories into five developmental sections.They are:

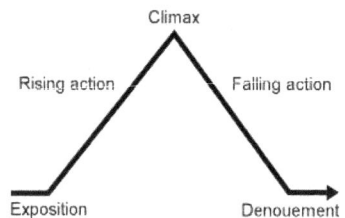

1) Introduction: Often referred to as the exposition. Here, any background information needed to properly understand the story is revealed to the audience.

2) Rising Action: The story becomes a little more complicated as dangers or conflicts are introduced. Often, this is made more interesting when a primary conflict is then complicated by the introduction of a secondary conflict.

3) Climax: The climax is the point of the story that is meant to peak the audience's interests the most. It is the part where all the action happens, often as a major turning point for the characters.

4) Falling Action: This is for the characters to resolve any remaining items that may still need closure. The main part of the story has thus concluded and the story is headed toward the end. This may often contain a moment of final suspense where the final outcome of the conflict is still in doubt.

5) Dénouement, Resolution, or Catastrophe: This is the final ending of the story where any conflicts or tensions have been resolved and the characters usually return to a 'normal' life. In a dénouement, the characters are set to be better off than they were at the beginning of the story; in a catastrophe, the characters are set to be worse off than they were previously (often the death of several main characters). A resolution simply returns life back to normal (most times).

The five-act story structure is best suited situations where there is a little more time for a more vivid story (3 minutes or more), and may be used with myths, fables, folk-tales and fairy-tales. If you have the listener's attention, and there is time to spare, you will gain a deeper sense of rapport and build a more emotional involvement with the 5-act story structure.

Literary Devices – Storytelling Techniques

Story techniques are used to make a story more interesting. The following is a list of common storytelling techniques:

Narrative Hooks:

A narrative hook is a section at the beginning of the story that gets the reader or audience aroused and interested, thus wanting to continue engaging in the story.

> "Have you ever wondered why you can't get what you want in life? Listen up, and we'll discuss the 8 things you MUST do to achieve personal success!"

The Aside

The aside is when you steps outside of the story itself and speaks directly to the listener. For example:

If the story is about you, then during the story you may create a short break in the story itself and speak directly to the listener, returning to finish the story afterwards.

> "Just yesterday I spent Christmas with my nieces and nephews, and it dawned on me how different life is today… [Aside begins] Back when I was a child there was the children spent more time playing together in the outdoors, today, technology controls the minds of our youths [Aside ends]"

Backstory

A story is often told without completely disclosing the background that led to the events of the story itself. This can leave the listener without a full understanding of the narrative, so in order to rectify this, the background may be told prior to the story itself or possibly even within the story (essentially creating a break within the story). It is also possibly to divide backstories into several parts or mini-sections that are told in relevant sections of the story itself.

"The reason George is like that is because when he was young his father use to scold him a lot for things that were out of his control… Over many years he has lost his sense of self-worth"

Chekhov's Gun

This is the introduction of something (anything) early in the story whose meaning is left unclear until later on. Anton Chekhov, a German physician and author (also considered to be one of the greatest short story writers in history), once said:

"Remove everything that has no relevance to the story. If you say in the first chapter that there is a rifle hanging on the wall, in the second or third chapter it absolutely must go off. If it's not going to be fired, it shouldn't be hanging there."

"As we walked down the halls at school at 9pm, the school had just been cleaned by the janitor. It was so clean that not a single spec of dirt was noticeable, except a yellow banana peel lying on the ground, probably part of the janitor's lunch. … … … [Later in the story] Sure, we were wrong to try to hack the school's computer to change our grades, and found ourselves running from security down the hall. I had forgotten about the yellow banana peel on the ground… As my foot hit the banana peel I went flying into the air"

The Cliffhanger

The cliffhanger is a story ending that is designed to leave the listener in trapped in suspense. Essentially, this occurs when the ending of the story is in fact unfinished or left to the imagination of the listener. In conversation, this is sure to cause a sense of desire in the listener to know more about the ending, and he will surely ask question, which in turns gets him involved in more conversation.

> "It was almost over, and certain that we had gotten a passing grade, we handed our assignments to the teacher and awaited her review!" [Used as an ending to the story].

Discovery

This occurs when a character of the story realizes something that was previously unknown, causing the story to take a sudden turn or twist.

> "I didn't want to do it… Just the thought of speaking in public frightened me… My anxiety got anxiety. But without choice I stumbled to the front of the stage and fought to force my eyes open. I struggled to start the first sentence. I started moving my body vigorously with every phrase. And you know what I found… They loved me… I had captured the audience like no other presenter could. Even more importantly, I loved it too."

Exposition

Exposition is a short introduction of the story that brings the listener up to speed on the current situation to where the story actually begins. It may also be used mid-story to speed up the story itself, leaving out insignificant details.

"In order to understand why the following events were so important to me, you must first understand the state of economy in my home town… We were poor folks with little money, shabby homes, and no future."

Flashbacks

The flashback (also called an analysis) is used to interrupt the normal development of the story to bring the listener back in time for a short moment. It can also be used to bring clarification to the main part of the story by informing the listener of past events in the lives of the character(s) within the story. The flashback can also be used to connect together events that are related, but yet separated in time.

"As every living moment I had was spent studying the fine art of communication, I remembered how lazy I was in school, how I refrained from studying or doing homework in those days… Ahhh, if only I'd been more studious then, maybe things would be easier now."

Flash-forward

The natural progression of the story is temporarily interrupted and the listener is brought forward in time for a short period, returning to the main story shortly. It is usually used to show future probabilities or possibilities, or otherwise to purvey plausible cause and effects of what may happen if the character in the story does certain things.

"These skills will help you become a better communicator, so that you can get what you want out of life… Can you imagine it now: Negotiating for that raise in pay; swaying beautiful women; building better relationships?"

Fold

This occurs when the story suddenly takes a different direction. In effect, the story begins once again from the current situation. This usually has the effect of leaving the listener guessing what will happen next.

> "I was walking through Chinatown, when I noticed a man looking at me strangely; I looked away and noticed another man was also staring at me. It's as if I was in the place at the wrong time… And before I knew it, a massive parade broke out on that street, with dancing lions and firecrackers, and lots of performers."

Foreshadowing

Foreshadowing is when we leave clues or indications about what will happen later in the story. The goal is to give the listener pieces that don't quite fit together while still hinting at the plausible importance of those pieces. This technique is often used more than once in a connected stream of foreshadowing called 'multiple foreshadowing'. There are several ways of foreshadowing events, such as: The use of flash-forward as foreshadowing; mention of worry, apprehension or heightened concern earlier in the story; predictions; or symbolism.

> "I thought my troubles over, but a little voice inside my head had mentioned that the worst is yet to come…"

In Medias Res

This literally means "in the middle of things". It is the act of beginning the story in the middle of where it is logical to start the story from. This allows the audience to dive right into a story and gets them to wonder 'what happened' previously.

> "It happened to me last week… Bam!!! Just like that. I was in a situation that I knew I couldn't handle. The crowd was asking me questions I didn't have answers to. The only way I could get out of it was by passing the buck on to someone else"

The MacGuffin

The McGuffin is an object, event, or thing that appears to be the central focus at first but is actually unimportant to the story as a whole. It is often used to introduce another situation or otherwise to introduce characters or objects.

> "I crept into the room, and noticed a coffee table. On the coffee table were a newspaper, a wine glass, and a paper clip. I searched book shelf for the secret book, and when I finally found the book, it had a small lock holding shut. I realized I could use the paper clip to open the lock"

Chapter 9

Can I Ask You A Question?

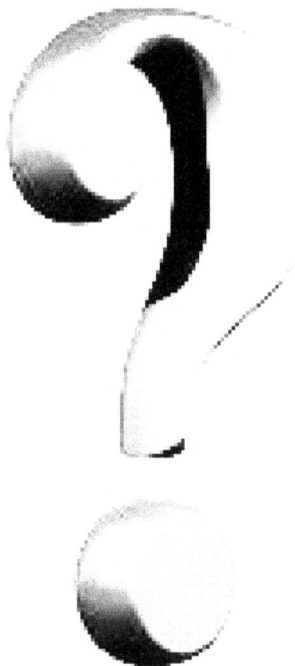

*Discover The Power of
Asking Great Questions*

*W*hen I engage in a conversation with the intention of achieving a particular result, I spend less than 15% of the conversation speaking. That is, I try to allow the other person in the conversation to do most of the speaking. There are many reasons for this, which you will soon find... The main reason is that when they walk away from the conversation, I want them to think "God, I like that guy, that was a wonderful conversation!" I mean, let's face it, how could they possibly not enjoy the conversation if they were doing most of the talking!

When you ask someone a question, it grabs their attention; it pulls their concentration toward you as they attempt to satisfy your question. It gets them involved in a conversation, and getting them involved with you is part of building a good relationship. More importantly, questions allow you to uncover the needs, desires, and beliefs of your client, as well as other important information that will allow you to further the relationship and move forward in the conversation. The key is asking the right questions at the right moment.

Questions also allow you to:

1) Control and lead your client to the decisions you want them to make.

2) Isolate areas of interest or decision trigger points.

3) Acknowledge facts (such as facts that are used to lead them to a decision).

4) Receive minor agreements.

5) Arouse and control emotion.

6) Isolate objections or areas of concern.

7) Lead the client into answering their own questions and/or objections.

8) Instill indirect suggestions or otherwise get your client to think about and/or consider things they may not have considered.

Effective Questioning

To be effective, questions need to be thought out. There are five requirements that all questions should follow:

1) Have A Purpose: Effective questions should be designed to elicit a specific response. The desired response may be verbal or non-verbal and it may be thoughtful or emotional.

2) Be Understood: The question needs to be understood by the receiver as it was intended.

3) Be Directed:

4) Be Specific: Effective questions are designed and expressed with specificity in mind. We covered specificity in chapter 6.

5) Preclude Guessing: Largely through the use of specificity, effective questions should prevent the listener from having to guess what was said or what was meant by the question.

Main Classifications of Questions

Below is a list of some main classifications of questions… Other question types may be considered subcategories of these classifications. For example: W-H questions include any type of question that focuses on words, such as whom, what, when, why, etc., but "challenging questions" also include these and may thus be considered W-H questions. This may not be a complete list of classifications:

W-H Questions

There are a series of different classifications of questions referred to as W-H questions because they begin with these letters (with the exception of how). The main six W-H questions are who, what, where, when, why, and how. Other forms of W-H questions may include which, whose, and whom.

Open-Ended vs. Close-Ended Questions

Question forms can essentially be broken down into two forms, and all other question forms stem from this:

1) Open-Ended Questions: Open-ended questions are those that allow the listener to answer without restrictions. The answer can be long or short and allows for a full dialogue of conversation.

2) Close-Ended Questions: Close-ended questions are those in which there are a limited number of possible answers.

Convergent vs. Divergent Questions

1) Convergent: Any type of question can be a convergent question as long as it is designed to accept only one correct answer. Common question forms that are used for convergent questioning include multiple choice, definitions, true or false, fill in the blank, and calculations where there is only one correct answer.

Sometimes convergent questions may work on the principle of ideology, meaning the question can be answered in any manner as long as the concept or idea supporting the answer is the same. For example: if you were asked, "Where were you born?" the answer, essentially, would be the same regardless of the specific words that you used to answer the question. (i.e. "I was born in Toronto, Ontario" vs. "I was born Ontario's largest metropolitan city, Toronto").

2) Divergent: Divergent questions are the opposite of convergent questions (listed above). Divergent questions have no correct answer and are designed to get the client to synthesize information, open up, provide an opinion, or create a hypothesis.

Dichotomous vs. Multiple Choice Questions

1) Dichotomous: Also referred to as "alternative choice questions", these are fixed questions that can only be answered in one of two ways. Examples of dichotomous questions include: yes or no, true or false, and right or wrong.

2) Multiple Choice Questions: These are questions that provide three or more possible answers. The possible answers are often fixed, meaning they are pre-determined by the questioner.

Types of Questions

When asking questions, there should be some underlying goal or reason for asking the question – whether that be to acquire information, further the conversation, persuade or influence, or solicit some type of cognitive or emotional response. Below you will find a list of different question types to aid you in achieving those goals.

Active Questions

Also referred to as "involvement questions", active questions require the client to be in the frame of mind of acting or doing something, or otherwise having previously acted. They effectively reframe or reposition the client's reality in their own mind. Examples include:

"How often will you use the product?"

"Who will be using the product most?"

"Where will you place your X ?"

Assumptive Questions

Assumptive questions are used when you assume that the responder already has the information or ability. Assumptive questions are often used to test a person's knowledge or otherwise to gain additional knowledge that may not have been readily offered – essentially gaining two pieces of information through one question. Take a look at the following sample question:

"Hey, Jason, where did John go?" (This question assumes that Jason knows where John went. We could have just asked "Jason, do you know where John went?", but the assumptive version is much more direct by assuming that Jason already knew where John went).

Let's look at another assumptive question: "Who else makes these kinds of decisions?" (The assumption here is that the responder is one of the people who make those decisions and that there are others who are also involved. If the responder does not make the decisions, he would be likely to say so and plausibly offer the name of the person who does).

Challenging Questions

Challenging questions are designed to challenge a decision made by the client. They generally begin with "Why is...?", "Why do...?", or "Why would...?" For example:

"Why is this the only way it could happen?"

"Why do you believe that?"

"Why would you prefer these widgets over those?"

Clarifying Questions

These questions are designed to get the client to clarify a previous statement. Examples include:

"What did you mean by...?"

"Can you clarify...?"

Comparative Questions

Comparative questions force the client to compare one thing against another. These could be two separate situations, objects, benefits, etc. Comparative questions usually start with the word "which".

"Which do you think is better…?"

"Do you prefer X or Y ?"

Confirmation Questions

The confirmation question is designed to answer a question asked by your client with a question that confirms their interest. For example: Let's say your client asks you if a product comes in a different color (let's say red), they would ask, "Does it come in red?" to which you would reply, "Would you like it in red?"

The "advanced confirmation question" would be to confirm the client has made the correct judgment; these questions usually begin with "Are you sure…?", "Are you certain…?", or some form of these. If the client asked, "Does it come in red", the advanced confirmation would then be "Are you sure red is the best color for your needs?"

Contingency Questions

Also referred to as "filtering questions" or "qualifying questions", these are questions that are asked in order to assist in determining if the client is qualified to respond to a second question.

Double Blind Questions

The double blind question is one in which the answer remains the same, regardless of whether it is answered negatively or positively (i.e. with a yes or a no response).

Embedded Questions

Embedded questions are not really questions at all. They are actually statements that contain an implied question that remains unasked but the answer of which remains desired. An example of an embedded question would be "I can't find my cell phone!" This statement contains the implied question of "Do you know where my cell phone is?"

Empowering Questions

Empowering questions seek to reduce the limitations of beliefs that people hold about a particular subject. They are used to clarify and help expand a person's thought process about their beliefs, values, opinions, etc. Examples include:

"What could change your current situation?"

"How else could that have been handled?"

"Is there anything else that you could do in this case?"

Evaluative Questions

These questions are designed to get the client to evaluate something, thus reducing the limitations of the beliefs that they hold about it. They are used to clarify and help expand a person's thought process about their beliefs, values, opinions, etc. Examples may include:

"Why do you think that?"

"What causes you to believe that?"

"How do you think that affects…?"

Feedback Questions

This question form is used by repeating the exact statement made by the client but in a questioning manner and tone of voice, forcing the client to explain their statement in further detail. The general idea is to act truly surprised by the client's statement so that when the client sees (or hears) your surprise, they will feel compelled to elaborate. This not only furthers the conversation but also forces the client to be more specific about their previous statement.

Inference Questions

These questions ask the responder to "fill in the blank" and insert missing information or otherwise make conclusions based on some other established information. These are often used to cause the responder to look beyond what is obvious. Examples of inference questions may include:

"What do you think is meant by…?"

"Why do you think that happened?"

"What might have happened if…?"

Interpretative Questions

Interpretive questions are questions designed to gain a better understanding of, or interpret, the meaning that is intended by the speaker. These questions will usually begin with some form of the following:

"What do you mean…?"

"Can you define…?"

"Why do you think…?"

Interrogative Questions

Interrogative questions use W-H questions in an interrogative manner (generally as direct questions)… Below are some examples:

"Who went there?"

"What time was it?"

"Why did you do that?"

Leading Questions

Leading questions are those that are designed to (attempt to) force the responder to answer with a pre-specified response. They are often designed using tag questions to entice the responder into the desired response. Most questions that use tag questions are actually leading questions. Leading questions may alternatively be designed as direct statements using a stress of inflection to turn the statement into a question.

An example of a leading question with a tag question would be: "You went out to the bar without me last night, didn't you?" The same leading question can be asked without the use of the tag question as follows: "You went out to the bar last night." The inflection can be stressed at "you", "went out", "the bar", or "last night", depending on the focus of the leading question (the words where the inflection is stressed would cause that part of the sentence to be the focus of the question).

Personal Questions

These are questions that are designed to extract information that may be considered personal to the responder. Some examples follow:

"What is your name?"

"How old are you?"

"What do you do in your leisure time?"

Provocative Questions

Provocative questions are designed to challenge what is already known or accepted.

The fast food restaurant Wendy's used a provocative question throughout North America in their 1984 commercial, the slogan being "Where's The Beef?" This catchphrase was designed to show how their hamburger had more beef than the competition.

Other examples of provocative questions may include:

"What is the purpose of this?"

"Is there anything useful in this book?"

"What the heck are you doing?"

"Are you tired of working 9 to 5?"

Reflective Questions

Reflective questions are designed to get the client to think about their reasoning, knowledge, feelings, or any aspect of their internal processing.

"How do you make those decisions?"

"What criteria do you look for?"

"How do you really feel when that happens?"

Rhetorical Questions

Rhetorical questions are questions to which a response is unneeded because the answer is already known to both the speaker and the listener.

Recall Questions

These are questions that ask the person answering to remember information from past experience. They often begin with phrases such as "Do you remember…?" or "Can you recall…?"

"Do you remember when you learned to ride a bike?"

"Can you recall the last time you bought a used car?"

Probing Questions

Probing questions are a category of questions designed to gather additional information about an answer to a previous question. They often use the interrogative question form (described above) and are designed to seek additional information that can be used to further the conversation on a particular topic.

Much like interrogative questions, probing questions make use of W-H questions (who, when, where, what, why, and how).

Some of the topics that you may want to consider probing for include:

1) Emotion: Why does the responder feel the way he does about a particular answer? (i.e. "Did that make you feel bad about the whole situation?")

2) Relevance: Ask how two things are connected, related, or relevant to each other. (i.e. "How does that relate to the current conversation?")

3) Elaboration: Ask for elaboration on the response that was given. (i.e. "Can you tell me more about that?")

4) *Completeness:* Ensure that all the information has been disclosed. (i.e. "Is there anything else you may have missed?")

5) *Concerns:* Ask about concerns, doubts, or objections. (i.e. "Do you think there may be a problem with that?")

Tag Questions

A tag question is a two- or three-word question that is added to the end of a statement or sometimes to the end of another question. These questions usually require simple one- or two-word responses such as "yes", "no", "it could", "I did", etc.

Tag questions, and the preceding statement, generally make use of modal verbs such as "would", "could", "should", "shall", etc.

There are two main forms of tag questions, they are:

1) *Balanced Tag Question:* Balanced tag questions use an opposite polarity for statement and its associated tag question, which means if the statement is of a positive form, then the associated tag question will be of a negative form (i.e. "You want to know more, don't you?")

Balanced tag questions are applied to force the responder to respond in a desired manner. Examples include:

"You did think it was crazy, didn't you?"

"You do want this new widget, don't you?"

2) *Unbalanced Tag Questions:* Unbalanced tag questions use a similar polarity for both the statement and its associated tag question, meaning if the statement is of a positive form, then the associated tag question will also be of a positive form. Below are some examples:

"You want to know more, do you?"

"We both understand what it feels like, don't we?"

Unbalanced tag questions are designed to apply additional emphasis on the question itself.

* Tag questions may also be categorized by type, meaning by the result they wish to achieve. The difference is in the intention of the speaker. Below are a few types of tag questions.

1) Inquisitive Tag Questions: These are tag questions designed to inquire about something. For example: "He is doing well in school, isn't he?"

2) Declarative Tag Questions: Often referred to as "exclamatory tag questions", these are tag questions designed to make a statement. For example: "That is a great vacation, isn't it?"

3) Assumptive Tag Questions: The assumptive tag question is an inquisitive tag question that attempts to confirm an assumptive statement. An example of this would be: "You would do a better job, wouldn't you?"

4) Erroneous Conclusion Tag Questions: This tag question is pre-stated by making a statement that is obviously false and then using a tag question in an attempt to confirm the obviously false statement. Under particular circumstances, this type of question may help reduce resistance as it may give the appearance of being comical or rhetorical. Below are two examples:

"None of us would like to have more money, would we?"

"We couldn't make things better if we tried, could we?"

Chapter 10

Creative Conversation

Add Style To Your Conversation!

*T*hroughout history, there have been men and women who, through conversation and public speaking, have been able to not only captivate the hearts of others, but attract the masses with creative speech. Those speeches influenced, motivated, drove and inspired others... To never know that words alone could produce such power. In this chapter, we review a host of techniques that may be used to turn ordinary conversational speech into something more...

Active & Passive Voices

Active and passive voices are methods of making a phrase or sentence appear more exciting or action-oriented., or less exciting or action-oriented.

Active Voice

In the active voice, the subject is performing the action (the verb). The subject could be a person or an object or a place. The subject is always disclosed before the verb (not after it). The active voice often provides an incline in emotion as it is heard. An example of active voice would be:

"John quickly opened the door."

In the above example, "John" is the subject. John performed an action (he opened the door).

Passive Voice

In the passive voice, the subject is not the one performing the action (the verb), rather the action is being performed to the subject (someone or something is performing the action). The action (the verb) is written before the subject. The passive voice is best used when the action or verb is more important than the subject, and a lack of dynamics is required and often provides a decline in emotion as it is heard.

Compare the following sentence to the one used above in the active voice:

"The door was quickly opened by John."

You'll find the focus of the statement was moved away from John, and here (in the passive voice), the focus in put on the fact that the door was opened, not on the person opening it.

Passive voice is a wonderful tool to aid in removing blame… Instead of saying "I turned it on and it broke", you can move blame away from you by saying "It broke when I turned it on". In the first statement it appears that the method in which "it" was turned on is the cause of it breaking. In the second statement, the fault is made to appear like a mechanical problem, and "it" would have broken regardless of how it was turned on.

Emphasis

We've spoke a bit about emphasis throughout this book… But what exactly does it mean to add emphasis to a word? Well… Emphasis is created by altering the normal sound of a word in some fashion. This can be done by changing the dynamics (volume and ambiance), the tonality, or the inflection (pitch) of your voice when speaking that particular word. Emphasis may also be added by speaking words in an elongated fashion, or stretching the spoken word out.

Why would we do this? Good question... Adding emphasis to a particular word within a phrase or sentence causes the listener, whether consciously or unconsciously, to become more attentive to that word, or possibly even to focus on that particular word. By getting the listener to focus on one particular word within a sentence, the remainder of the words within that sentence become de-emphasized, or appears less important. This in turn causes us to believe that the emphasized word has some type of significance.

In the sentence above "The door was quickly opened by John", we can emphasize one word – such as "was", and now the sentence "The door <u>was</u> quickly opened by John" appears to declare a fact... It certainly was opened by John; there is no doubt about that!

In most cases, when using statements, emphasizing a word will change that word into a declaration. However, that may not always be the case. As you speak, consider how the emphasis on particular words alters the impression of the words/phrases you use.

Verbs

The use of the right verbs can make a drastic difference in how your communication is accepted, interpreted and understood. Verbs not only tell the listener what happened, but how it happened.

Action Verbs

Action verbs show the subject of the sentence performing some action. This can be very powerful when used in the right context. While regular verbs are used in our general everyday conversation, action verbs (often synonyms of regular verbs) are used to add more excitement, dramatic appeal and/or illustration.

Consider, for example, the difference between the following two sentences.

"He worked night and day to finish the task".

"He slaved night and day to accomplish the task".

As you can see, there is a difference between "working" and "slaving"; as there is between finishing something and accomplishing something (accomplishing suggests some gain afterward, while finishing simply means it has been completed). The use of the action verbs "slaving" and "accomplishing" make the statement more emotive. Below is a short list of action verbs:

Accentuate	Amplify	Attribute	Augment
Broaden	Characterize	Conceal	Configure
Construct	Defy	Denounce	Diagnose
Elaborate	Emphasize	Engage	Exhibit
Expose	Express	Feature	Grasp
Highlight	Identify	Illustrate	Instigate
Intensify	Manipulate	Misconceive	Negate
Obstruct	Perceive	Position	Propose
Reconfigure	Reconstruct	Refrain	Reveal
Stimulate	Sustain	Transform	Trigger
Validate	Witness		

Let's transform an ordinary every day sentence using some of these action verbs: Instead of saying

"You can do one thing and become good at it, or you can do many things and become great"... You could say

"You can focus on one area and highlight how good you are, or you can engage in a multitude of skills and broaden your horizons to reveal your own greatness"... I like the second one better, don't you?

State-of-Being Verbs

These are usually some state of the verb "is"; they literally describe a state of being. Such verbs are less powerful than action verbs, and are often used to precede another verb. These include:

Be	Is	Am	Are
Was	Were		

You can use state-of-being verbs to add extra emphasis to the fact that something is being done. When doing this, be certain to stress the state-of-being verb. For instance: "We are studying for the test".

There/It Introductions

Beginning a sentence with the words "there" or "it" followed by a state-of-being verb, is generally not recommended. These types of sentenced introductions only postpone the beginning of the actual sentence, thus complicating the sentence without cause. Below is a short list of these introductions:

There is	There are	There was

The following are two examples of There/It introductions, including both faulty and correct methods of beginning a sentence:

1a) Faulty: There was a chapter in the book that described verbs.

1b) Correct: A chapter in the book described verbs.

2a) Faulty: It is a perfect beginning to a wonderful story.

2b) Correct: The beginning of the story is wonderful.

Descriptive Language

Descriptive language is the use of words that help build mental images in the mind of the listener. These mental images help the listener to form a better picture in their mind of the ideas that you wish for them to understand, and when successive imagery is created, you may even form a sort of motion picture in their minds… The better they can form these pictures, the more involved they will be as a listener.

Descriptive language makes use of words that evoke the senses (sight, sound, smell, taste, and touch); as well as the emotions and state of the listener. It makes use of adjectives and adverbs. Action verbs may also be significant to the overall meaning of a phrase or sentence. Read more about this below:

Adjectives

Adjectives are words that evoke the five senses. They describe nouns (people, places, things, etc.) or pronouns (generic words that can take the place of a noun – such as he, she, they, it, each, somebody, etc.).

1) Sight: Use words that tell above colors, shapes, and sizes. For example:

"The ugly car was <u>big</u> and <u>blue</u>, and also <u>box-shaped</u>".

2) Sound: Use words that describe the type of sound (i.e. crash, thunder, bang, etc.), and degrees of volume (i.e. loud, soft, ear-threatening, etc.). You may also use words that tell about the result that occurs from the sound. For example:

"She <u>yelled</u> at me so furiously as to <u>deafen</u> me forever".

3) Smell: Use words that describe scent (i.e. "the smell of roses"); or the strength of the smell (i.e. strong, faint, bear, etc.). For example:

"Her <u>perfume faintly</u> smelled like <u>wild roses in the cool breeze</u>.

4) Taste: Use of words or phrases that describe flavor (i.e. sweet, sour, spicy, etc.), or potency (strong, weak, bland, etc.).

"The <u>sweet</u> taste of <u>chocolate melting</u> in my mouth was a godsend on this tiresome day.

5) Touch: Use of words or phrases that describe textures (i.e. smooth, rough, soft, etc.), and temperature (hot, warm, cool, cold, etc.).

"I <u>felt</u> her <u>rubbing</u> her hand upon my back so as to sooth my cough."

6) Emotions: Use of words that describe emotions (i.e. happy, sad, excited, lonely, etc.).

"I was <u>ecstatic</u> to see how well you were progressing; you have really been improving well."

7) State of Being: Use of words that describe the state of a person or thing (i.e. tired, bored, crazy, etc.).

"I've been <u>persistent</u> in my learning, but now I am <u>very tired</u> and need some R & R."

Adverbs

Adverbs are words that change or modify the meaning of a verb (an action). Although they may be suited to modify other words, they are most commonly used with verbs. Adverbs provide additional information that not only change the notion of the entire phrase, but also place more attention on the verb. Consider the following two phrases:

"He worked <u>swiftly</u>."

"He worked <u>slowly</u>."

In the two sentences above, the adverbs "swiftly" and "slowly" modify how the person ran. In the context of the overall sentence, this can make a dramatic difference… "He worked <u>swiftly</u> to get things done on time". You can see how this is different than simply stating "He worked to get things done on time".

When combined with intensifiers, adverbs increase their effect… Compare the following statement to the one above: "He worked <u>very swiftly</u> to get the job done".

Manner

Adverbs of manner describe how something is done/performed. The adverb should normally be placed behind the noun or object of the sentence (i.e. "He placed the box [object] carefully [adverb] on the shelf"). Below is a list of some adverbs of manner:

Angrily	Anxiously	Badly
Beautifully	Carefully	Carelessly
Cautiously	Deliberately	Easily
Quickly	Happily	Innocently
Kindly	Mysteriously	Naturally
Nervously	Patiently	Perfectly
Powerfully	Quickly	Reluctantly
Repeatedly	Slowly	Well

Adverbs of manner are well suited to emphasize a statement, adding additional power to the verb they modify.

Place

These are adverbs that describe location. As with adverbs of manner, these should be placed behind the noun or object of the phrase (i.e. I don't see the car [object] anywhere [adverb]"). Below is a short list of adverbs of place:

Away	Back / Backward	Behind
Below	Downstairs	Elsewhere
Far	Here	Inside
Near / Nearby	Off	On
Out	Over	There
Towards	Under	Up
Where		

Frequency

These are adverbs that tell or ask how many times, or how often, something is done. These adverbs should be placed directly before the main verb. A short list of adverbs of frequency is provided below:

Always	Frequently	Generally
Hardly (ever)	Infrequently	Never
Normally	Occasionally	Often
Rarely	Regularly	Seldom
Sometimes	Usually	

These adverbs are suited for emphasizing or de-emphasizing certain verbs or phrases.

Time

Adverbs of time describe when something was done. They are usually placed at the end of a sentence (i.e. I worked yesterday). Below is a short list:

Now	Then	Today
Tomorrow	Tonight	yesterday
Early	Eventually	Finally
First	Just	Last
Late	Next	Previously
Recently	Since	Soon
Still	Yet	

Purpose

Often referred to as adverbs of cause or adverbs of reason, these adverbs describe why something is happening or is done.

Hence	Thus	Therefore
Accordingly	Consequently	Ergo
Subsequently		

Degree

Adverbs of degree describe the extent to which something is done. Adverbs of degree should be placed just before the verb they modify (i.e. "He <u>almost</u> finished everything"). Below is a list of adverbs of degree:

Almost	Absolutely	Barely
Completely	Deeply	Enough
Entirely	Extremely	Fairly
Fully	Greatly	Hardly
Highly	Incredibly	Just
Little	Mostly	Nearly
Practically	Scarcely	Somewhat
Virtually		

Conjunctions

Conjunctions are words that join two sentences or two clauses together. The most common type of conjunctions are called coordinating conjunctions. There are seven coordinating conjunctions:

And   Nor   But   Or   So   Yet

However   For

> You can use a conjunction in your sentences, stretching out the vowel sound of the conjunction in order to give you time to think of what to say next. This prevents the listener from thinking that you have finished speaking.

Discourse Markers

Discourse markers work much in the same way that conjunctions do… As a matter of fact, many conjunctions are used as discourse markers. A discourse marker is a word or phrase used at the beginning of a phrase or sentence, and may be used to join two sentences together They are imported from other classes of words, such as conjunctions, adjectives, adverbs, etc.

Discourse markers may also be used at the end of a sentence to instigate turn-taking, or to suggest to the speaker to either continue speaking or to elaborate on what has already been said. When we say something, for instance, and end our sentence with "so…" we are telling the other person to continue, or to continue where we left off. The same goes for such words as "and", "okay…", or "like…" Some common discourse markers are provided below:

You know	Like	Actually
Basically	I mean	Okay,
On the other hand	While	Where as
However	Nevertheless	Mind you
Still	Yet	In Spite of this
In the same way	Of course	Certainly
In particular	As a result	Consequently
So	Then	Moreover
Furthermore	In addition	And another thing
Generally	In general	Broadly speaking

Example: <u>Okay</u>, so yesterday was the best day of my life. <u>Of course</u>, it didn't start out that way. <u>Generally</u>, my days never start out very good, until I have that first cup of coffee. <u>Certainly</u>, <u>however</u>, there is always room for deviance, and that's what happened yesterday.

In the above example, I used five discourse markers in this one paragraph of text… Most people do not use discourse markers so frequently. You will also notice in the use of "Certainly, however" that discourse markers may often be stacked, generally with no more than two discourse markers in sequence.

Strategic Silence

While speech is important, as is the choice of the right words and phrases for every situation, so too, does silence have great qualities. Sometimes, it is best not to say anything at all.

Silence can be eloquent, meaning that is serves a function, and should be considered a relevant part of any communicative act. It plays a part in communicating messages just as speech does. In this sense, it is called eloquent silence. In music and poetry, this eloquent silence is called a "caesura", and is defined as "a complete pause in a line of poetry and/or in a musical composition". Below are several ways in which it may do this in speech:

Discourse Marker

Above we spoke about discourse markers, and how they are often used to join two sentences. Silence may also be used in such a manner. We may use silence in our own speaking, so to leave a pause as the joining of two sentences (often combined with some form of body-

> Without The Polarity of Silence, The System of Language Would Fall.
> -   *Susan Sontag*

language); or we may use silence as a means of instigating turn-taking.

Grammatik Marker

My favorite use of silence is that of a Grammatik marker. When we read a passage from a piece of literature, we find marks of grammar that set one phrase or sentence apart from another… Such marks of grammar also indicate pause or silence:

1) Silence as Parenthesis: Parenthesis is used for information that does not follow the natural flow of your sentence, but that needs to be included anyway. Parentheses are often used to provide additional information that clarifies or supplements something already said. In writing, parenthesis is signified by the use of brackets, in speech, however, it is signified through the use of a short pause before and after the parenthesis.

2) Silence as Ellipse or Dash: An ellipse, in writing, is a set of three consecutive dots used to signify an extended pause. A dash has the same effect, but usually to a shorter degree. Dashes, however, generally unlike the ellipse, are often used before and after a phrase so as to set it apart from the rest of the sentence (possibly as emphasis).

3) Silence After Commas or Periods: A period signifies the end of a phrase or sentence, or otherwise the completion of a stream of thought. As it signifies an ending it is only natural that there should be a stop or pause after periods.

4) Silence After Exclamation: The exclamation mark is probably the most powerful marker in grammar. It signifies a rising of expression. An emotional surge. Excitement!

With the rise of emotion must come a stop, similar to the pause after a period, except the pause after an emotional statement is generally a bit longer as to give the reader a moment to catch his breathe.

Speech Act

If we remember from chapter 1, a speech act is the act of saying something through speech, other than the literary meaning of the speech. It encompasses the intent of the speaker. Silence, also, can take on form by way of the intent of the speaker… When one person speaks to another, and the second person purposely does not reply, it often means "I'm angry at you". However, if being asked for approval on a particular subject, it can also mean "I disapprove!" On the brighter side of things, imagine two lovers sitting at a park bench enjoying the sunset together…No words are needed for mutual understanding – It is clear that the silence of both people is effectively saying "I'm happy to be with you right now".

Silence can provide great insight into the thoughts of others, whether it is excitement, mourning, reverence, or astonishment. In each of these, it must be understood how the context of the situation affects the individual who is silent. Other considerations such as previous statements, body-language and other nonverbal language may also be taken into account.

Indicating Response

Silence can be an indication of response, especially in response to a direct question. For example: A judge in a court of law may ask a question to the respondent… To answer in silence, the respondent would be conceding guilty.

As another example: A husband and wife walk into a lady's fashion store… The wife says "Do you like this dress?", and the man doesn't answer. A response is given.

Requesting Response

Silence often terrifies people. In an interpersonal situation, where no one speaks and there is a sense of dead silence (a complete lack of noise), one person is bound to begin talking sooner or later. When a question is asked, and the listener does not respond, the same sense of dead silence can be felt. In such a case, the speaker often breaks the silence by continuing to speak, either by adding additional information and returning to request an answer, or possibly accepting no response and changing the subject to a different topic. What would happen though, if the speaker simply waited for a reply…? The listener would eventually say something!

Withholding Information

Silence can also be a means of withholding information. To plead the fifth, in the United States, means to say nothing. When somebody asks a question, you have the option of answering it in full; provide only a partial answer, or not answering at all. Depending on the context, you may have a strategic advantage in choosing one option over the other. The art of information manipulation, however, is a subject far too great for the likes of this book.

Emotive Language

Emotive language is the use of words that provoke some type of emotional response. If you really want to captivate people and pull their attention in towards you, you must aim to get them emotionally involved in the conversation.

Emotive language makes use of descriptive language as discussed above... With a special emphasis on adjectives that describe emotions (i.e. happy, sad, excited, lonely, etc.).

In the context of emotive language, all words can be thought of as divided into two main categories:

1) Denotation: The denotative meaning of a word is the actual or literary meaning of the word itself. This is fairly synonymous with the explicit meaning of words as discussed in chapter 4.

2) Connotation: The connotative meaning of a word is the essential idea that the word represents, generally in the view of the majority (of the people). This is similar to the implicit meaning of words as described in chapter 4.

Just to ensure understanding of this, let's look at a quick scenario: If I was to give a yellow rose to a friend, and say "I appreciate you", the yellow rose would signify good friendship; this is the connotation of a yellow rose as generally understood by the vast majority. If, however, the rose was red, the red rose would signify a stronger interpersonal relationship – Such as that between lovers.

In the use emotive language, we restructure our phrases so that the most emotionally implicit meaning of a word is used, instead of the explicit or denotative meaning. Consider the following:

"A house is just a structure; but a home is where you hang your hat".

The connotative meaning of words change the way in which the entire sentence is perceived through ideology (using words as ideas rather than the literal significance). It evokes an emotional response... The word "child" has a different meaning to most people, then the word "kid" (child relates to closeness and innocence, while "kid" simply refers to person who is not an adult, and could be of any age between 1 week and twenty years)... To elaborate on this, it is more likely that we would say call our own child "a child", and someone else's child "A kid" because the emotional involvement is greater with our own children, and significantly less with someone else's.

The word "woman" may refer to any female over the age of 20 years; while the word "lady" tends to refer to a woman of royal or similar class. The word "complete" simply refers to all pieces being accounted for; while the word "system" refers to a complete set that works together to provide specified results.

Learn to grow your vocabulary of synonyms, and reconsider the denotative and connotative meaning of words – Understand the impact of the words you use on your listeners. Use sentences that promote the connotative meaning when you want to excite an emotional response.

Figure of Speech

A figure of speech is a word, phrase or sentence that is designed to create an effect of some sort. Many figures of speech have become commonplace in day-to-day conversation, while others appear to be more confined to literature, and others yet are not often used at all. Below,

I've included only those that are commonly appropriate for spoken conversation.

Anaphora

Anaphora occurs when at the first part of a sentence is repeated in the second part of the same sentence. Sometimes, a word is changed so that it doesn't sound so much like a repetition. See the example below:

"Everybody likes winners, but nobody likes losers"

Cliché

A cliché is an expression that has been over-used, so that it has lost its expressive power. Examples include:

"Turn over a new leaf"

"A rose by any other name would still smell as sweet"

Hyperbole

This is the use of exaggerations for the purpose of amplifying a given statement. Most people use hyperbole naturally in day to day language. For example, if a task takes 5-6 hours to complete, we may say "It took the whole day" (did it really take the whole day?).

Hyperbole may be used to add humor to a conversation; or it may be used to add a sense of seriousness to the message.

Idiom

An idiom is a common expression that has come to mean something other than its literary meaning. Common Idioms include:

"It's raining cats and dogs"

"That cost me an arm and a leg"

Much like clichés, idioms have become common because of their over-use. Like clichés, idioms should be avoided.

Innuendo

Innuendo involves opinions, remarks or terminology that insinuates or provides subtle or indirect observation about a person or thing, usually of a salacious, critical, or wrongful nature. Examples of innuendo include: He was shooting his mouth off, and killed the conversation; or "He's not the smartest nail in the bunch".

Innuendo can be used to add humor to a conversation when speaking about events or inanimate objects. Innuendo should be avoided when referring to people to avoid future complications in relations.

Litote

This is a figure of speech in which an understatement is used for rhetorical effect, usually by using double negatives. Example: "He's not the most intelligent person in the world". (Meaning he's stupid).

Litotes may be commonly used amongst friends in a non-professional environment; but should be avoided in professional conversation as they devalue the subject of the conversation.

Metaphor

Metaphor is a very common figure of speech in where one word is equated to another or where one word is used to signify another, usually in an idealistic fashion. Metaphors often use comparative words to relate one thing to another. For example: the use of the phrase "broken heart" to suggest that a person is hurt and sad, however, the heart itself is not actually broken.

Because people often use comparisons to understand new ideas, metaphors can be used in explanation or to help reinforce a message (so others can comprehend the message better).

Metonymy

This occurs where one word is called by one of its associated words or ideas instead of calling it by its own name or instead of calling it what it really is.

A famous example of the use of metonymy is the phrase "The pen is mightier than the sword" ("pen" referring the writing skills, and "sword" referring to the use of force)

Another example is to say: "I need a **hand** with my suitcases" *("hand" refers to help)*. As another example: "Wall Street" is often used to refer to the U.S. financial sector; and "Hollywood" is used to refer to the U.S. major motion picture industry.

You can create your own metonymy, such that may be only understood between yourself and another person -The consistent use of which can help develop a relational bond. You can also use a commonly understood metonymy that is relevant to the conversation when you believe it would be understood by the listener, even if simply to change up your conversation .

Oxymoron

An oxymoron occurs when two terms are used together, that would ordinarily contradict each other.

Many oxymoron's are already a part of everyday speech or are commonly understood. Examples of oxymorons include: Clearly confused; act naturally; pretty ugly; alone together.

Because of their nature of including contradictory words, oxymoron may be used to add a hint of humor to the conversation. Place a stress or emphasis on the oxymoron when using them. Be careful, however, not to use oxymoron in a condescending manner.

Paradox

A paradox is a phrase or sentence that appears to contradict itself, but can be understood as not contradictory. Paradoxical statements often leave some room for debate.

A great example of a paradox, or paradoxical statement, would be to say "If this statement is true, then Santa Clause and the Tooth Fairy both exist". But the idea of Santa Clause and the Tooth Fairy exist, and to a child, a mother who exchanges a tooth under the pillow for money could essentially be considered "the tooth fairy"; and obviously the above statement exists, as you must have read it to understand my debate of the matter.

Paradoxical statements can be used to force someone to think deeper about a subject, think outside of the box of literary meaning, or otherwise to open intellectual debate about a conversation. Such statements should not be used otherwise.

Pun

A pun is a humorous comment that exploits words that have more than one meaning, or sometimes to exploit words that sound alike (homonyms and homophones).

An example of a pun would be "An elephant's opinion carries a lot of weight" (elephants also carry a lot of weight). Another example in response to the questions "Are you alright" may be "No, I'm half right, half left".

Puns can be used to add humor to a conversation. Before using puns, take note of the situational context, and the mood of the listener. Puns are best used when under a free-spirited and happy atmosphere.

Simile

A simile is a type of metaphor where two things are introduced as being similar (like the name says)... This is usually done using words such as "like", "as" or "its equivalent". In the movie 'Forrest Gump', Forrest uses a simile while sitting on the street bench talking to the old lady when he says "Life is like a box of chocolates, you never know what you'll get".

Like metaphors, similes can be effectively used in explanation or to help reinforce a message (so others can comprehend the message better).

Synecdoche

Synecdoche is a type of metonymy where a phrase or sentence uses words or terminologies that give a meaning similar or related to that which is literal in meaning, but is not meant exactly as is said. An example of synecdoche would be "Do you like my **wheels**?" (The word "wheels" refers to the entire vehicle).

> While synecdoche may be used to add a little spice to a conversation, it shouldn't be used too often, and may be considered a type of slang.

Tautology

In tautology, two or more words that are near-synonyms are placed together in context. For example: "Read the short summary about…", or "In my opinion, I think". In normal conversation, these figures of speech should not be used as they make conversation appear redundant, and lengthier than they need to be. Tautology can be created in two ways:

1) Successive Tautology: here, tautology is created when two words are used in succession, such as the examples above.

> Successive tautology does not add any apparent emphasis to a phrase and should generally be avoided because they make sentences appear too repetitive.

2) Non-Successive Tautology: Here, tautology is created using two similar words, but in two separate phrase. Take for example, to say "I am certain, and I do believe this is true."

Used effectively, this type of tautology can add emphasis and/or dramatic appeal to a sentence or phrase. Speak the tautology with an emphasis on the similar words. Do not use tautology too often.

Index Table

www.ingramcontent.com/pod-product-compliance
Lightning Source LLC
Chambersburg PA
CBHW060334200326
41519CB00011BA/1939